KIM MIA

BOISE

TRAVEL GUIDE

2025

Explore Top Attractions, Hidden Gems, and Outdoor Adventures in Idaho's Capital.

SCAN THIS QR CODE FOR PICTURES AND MAP

CONTENTS

CHAPTER 1: WELCOME TO BOISE
1.1 INTRODUCTION TO BOISE: THE CITY OF TREES

Welcome to Boise, a vibrant and dynamic city nestled in the heart of Idaho, affectionately known as the "City of Trees." Boise is a hidden gem that offers a perfect blend of urban sophistication and outdoor adventure, making it an ideal destination for tourists and visitors alike. Whether you're seeking a peaceful retreat, a taste of local culture, or an adrenaline-pumping adventure, Boise has something for everyone.

Boise's nickname, "The City of Trees," is more than just a moniker—it's a testament to the city's deep connection with nature. As you explore the city, you'll notice the lush green canopies that line its streets, parks, and neighborhoods. The Boise River, which meanders through the heart of the city, is surrounded by the Greenbelt, a 25-mile long tree-lined pathway that provides a serene escape for walkers, cyclists, and nature enthusiasts.

Boise's commitment to preserving its natural beauty is evident in its many parks and outdoor spaces. From the expansive Julia Davis Park to the tranquil Kathryn Albertson Park, you'll find countless spots to relax, picnic, and soak in the city's natural beauty. And if you're visiting in the fall, the city's tree-lined streets burst into a riot of autumn colors, creating a picturesque setting that's perfect for a leisurely stroll or a scenic drive.

Beyond its natural charm, Boise is rich in culture and history. The city's origins date back to the early 19th century when it was established as a fort to protect settlers and travelers. Today, Boise has grown into a thriving metropolis, while still maintaining its historic charm. The Old Idaho Penitentiary, the Basque Block, and the Idaho State Capitol are just a few of the historic sites that offer a glimpse into Boise's past.

The city is also a cultural hub, with a vibrant arts scene that includes everything from contemporary art galleries to historic theaters. The Boise

Art Museum, with its impressive collection of contemporary and regional art, is a must-visit for art lovers. Meanwhile, the city's thriving music and theater scenes offer something for every taste, whether you're interested in catching a live performance at the Morrison Center or exploring the local music scene at one of the many live music venues.

For outdoor enthusiasts, Boise is a gateway to adventure. The city is surrounded by stunning natural landscapes, offering endless opportunities for hiking, biking, fishing, and skiing. The nearby Boise Foothills are a playground for hikers and mountain bikers, with miles of trails that offer breathtaking views of the city and the surrounding mountains.

In the winter, Boise transforms into a snowy wonderland, with nearby Bogus Basin offering some of the best skiing and snowboarding in the region. And if you're looking for something more leisurely, the Boise River is perfect for a relaxing float or a day of fishing.

Boise's culinary scene is as diverse as its landscape, offering a wide range of dining experiences that reflect the city's rich cultural heritage. From farm-to-table restaurants that showcase the best of Idaho's local produce to authentic Basque cuisine that pays homage to the city's Basque heritage, Boise's food scene is sure to delight every palate.

Don't miss the Capital City Public Market, a bustling farmers' market where you can sample local delicacies, fresh produce, and artisanal goods. And for a taste of Boise's thriving craft beer scene, be sure to visit one of the many local breweries that dot the city.

One of the first things you'll notice about Boise is its friendly, welcoming atmosphere. The city's residents are known for their hospitality, and it won't take long for you to feel at home here. Whether you're exploring the historic downtown, taking a walk along the Greenbelt, or enjoying a meal at a local restaurant, you'll find that Boise is a city that's easy to navigate and even easier to fall in love with.

Boise's compact, walkable downtown is perfect for exploring on foot. From the historic 8th Street, with its eclectic mix of shops, cafes, and restaurants, to the scenic views from the Boise Depot, there's always something to discover around every corner.

1.2 HOW TO GET THERE

Boise, Idaho, is well-connected and easily accessible by various means of transportation. Whether you're flying in from another state or driving from a nearby city, getting to Boise is straightforward and convenient. Here's everything you need to know about the available travel options, flight and ticket booking, visa requirements, and getting to and from the airport.

BY AIR

1. Flights to Boise Boise is served by the Boise Airport (BOI), which is located just a few miles south of downtown. The airport is a regional hub that offers direct flights from major cities across the United States, including Los Angeles, Seattle, Denver, Chicago, Dallas, and more. Airlines such as Delta, United, Southwest, American, and Alaska Airlines operate daily flights to and from Boise, making it easy to find a convenient route.

2. Booking Flights Booking a flight to Boise is simple, with numerous online travel agencies and airline websites offering competitive prices and deals. Here are some popular websites where you can book flights and compare prices:

- **Expedia**: www.expedia.com

- **Kayak**: www.kayak.com

- **Google Flights**: www.google.com/flights

- **Skyscanner**: www.skyscanner.com

- **Airline Websites**: You can also book directly through the websites of major airlines like Delta, United, American, and Southwest.

When booking your flight, be sure to check for the best deals, consider flexible dates, and book in advance to secure the lowest prices.

3. Visa Requirements If you're traveling to Boise from outside the United States, you'll need to ensure you have the appropriate visa. For most international visitors, a valid U.S. visa is required. The type of visa you'll need depends on the purpose of your visit:

- **Tourist Visa (B-2)**: For those visiting Boise for tourism or leisure.

- **Business Visa (B-1)**: For business travelers attending meetings, conferences, or other professional events.

Some countries are part of the Visa Waiver Program (VWP), which allows their citizens to travel to the U.S. for tourism or business for up to 90 days without a visa. Check the U.S. Department of State website (www.travel.state.gov) for detailed information on visa requirements and to determine if your country is part of the VWP.

By Car

1. Driving to Boise For those who prefer road trips, Boise is accessible via major highways. Interstate 84 (I-84) runs through the city, connecting it to other major cities like Salt Lake City, Portland, and Seattle. The drive to Boise offers scenic views, especially if you're traveling through the mountains or desert landscapes.

- **From Salt Lake City**: Approximately 340 miles, about a 5-hour drive.

- **From Portland**: Approximately 430 miles, about a 6.5-hour drive.

- **From Seattle**: Approximately 500 miles, about a 7.5-hour drive.

Driving allows you to explore the surrounding areas at your own pace and is an excellent option for those looking to visit multiple destinations in the region.

2. Car Rentals If you're flying into Boise but want to explore the region by car, rental cars are available at the Boise Airport. Major rental agencies like Hertz, Avis, Enterprise, and Budget operate at the airport, providing a wide range of vehicles to suit your needs. Booking in advance is recommended, especially during peak travel seasons.

BY BUS OR TRAIN

1. Bus Services Boise is accessible by bus, with services provided by companies like Greyhound and other regional operators. Buses offer an affordable and comfortable way to reach Boise from nearby cities and states.

- **Greyhound**: Provides service to and from Boise with connections to various U.S. cities. Tickets can be booked online at www.greyhound.com.

2. Train Services Currently, there are no direct passenger train services to Boise. The nearest Amtrak stations are located in nearby cities such as Portland and Salt Lake City. From there, you can take a bus or drive to Boise.

GETTING TO THE AIRPORT

1. From Downtown Boise Boise Airport (BOI) is conveniently located about 4 miles from downtown, making it easy to reach by various means:

- **Taxi or Ride-Sharing**: Taxis and ride-sharing services like Uber and Lyft are readily available in Boise and can take you to the airport in about 10-15 minutes.

- **Public Transportation**: ValleyRide buses offer affordable transportation to and from the airport, with routes that connect the airport to downtown and other parts of the city.

- **Airport Shuttle**: Several hotels in Boise offer complimentary shuttle services to and from the airport for their guests.

2. Parking at Boise Airport If you're driving to the airport, Boise Airport offers several parking options, including short-term, long-term, and economy parking. Prices vary depending on the duration of your stay, and parking is conveniently located within walking distance of the terminal.

LEAVING THE AIRPORT

1. Ground Transportation Once you arrive at Boise Airport, getting to your final destination is easy:

- **Taxi and Ride-Sharing**: Taxis, Uber, and Lyft are available just outside the terminal. They offer quick and convenient transportation to downtown Boise and other areas.

- **Car Rentals**: If you've reserved a rental car, rental counters are located on the first floor of the parking garage, directly across from the terminal.

- **Public Transportation**: ValleyRide buses provide service from the airport to various parts of Boise, making it an affordable option for travelers.

2. Hotel Shuttles Many hotels in Boise offer complimentary shuttle services for guests arriving at the airport. Check with your hotel in advance to arrange for pick-up.

1.3 ESSENTIAL TRAVEL TIPS

When visiting Boise, Idaho, it's helpful to have some insider tips to ensure you make the most of your trip. Here's a guide to help you navigate the city with ease and enjoy your stay in the City of Trees.

1. BEST TIME TO VISIT

- **Spring (March to May)**: Spring is a great time to visit Boise when the weather is mild, and the city's trees and flowers are in full bloom. It's perfect for outdoor activities like hiking and biking.

- **Summer (June to August)**: Summer brings warm temperatures, ideal for enjoying the Boise River or attending outdoor festivals and events. Be prepared for higher hotel rates during peak tourist season.

- **Fall (September to November)**: Fall is beautiful in Boise, with cooler temperatures and vibrant autumn foliage. It's a great time for scenic drives and outdoor adventures.

- **Winter (December to February)**: Winters are cold, but if you enjoy skiing or snowboarding, this is the time to visit. Bogus Basin, just outside the city, offers excellent winter sports opportunities.

2. PACKING ESSENTIALS

- **Layers**: Boise's weather can be unpredictable, especially in spring and fall. Pack layers so you can adjust to changing temperatures throughout the day.

- **Comfortable Shoes**: Whether you're exploring the city or hitting the hiking trails, comfortable walking shoes are a must.

- **Sun Protection**: Summers in Boise can be hot, and the high altitude means stronger UV rays. Bring sunscreen, a hat, and sunglasses.

- **Reusable Water Bottle**: Boise is an outdoor-friendly city, and staying hydrated is important, especially during hikes or bike rides.

3. LOCAL TRANSPORTATION

- **Walking**: Downtown Boise is compact and pedestrian-friendly, making it easy to explore on foot.

- **Biking**: Boise is a bike-friendly city with many bike lanes and paths. You can rent bikes from various rental shops or use the city's bike-sharing program, Boise GreenBike.

- **Public Transit**: ValleyRide offers bus services that cover Boise and the surrounding areas. It's a convenient and affordable way to get around.

- **Ride-Sharing**: Uber and Lyft are widely available in Boise, providing an easy way to get around, especially if you're traveling outside the city center.

- **Car Rentals**: If you plan to explore beyond Boise, consider renting a car. It's the best way to visit nearby attractions like the Boise Foothills, Bogus Basin, and the Snake River.

4. SAFETY TIPS

- **General Safety**: Boise is known for being a safe city with friendly locals. Still, it's always wise to stay aware of your surroundings, especially at night.

- **Outdoor Safety**: When exploring the outdoors, let someone know your plans and carry a map, especially if you're heading into less populated areas. Stay on marked trails and bring plenty of water.

- **Wildlife**: Boise's proximity to nature means you may encounter wildlife, especially in parks and natural areas. Keep a safe distance from animals and don't feed them.

5. HEALTH AND WELLNESS

- **Altitude**: Boise sits at about 2,700 feet above sea level. If you're coming from sea level, give yourself time to adjust, and stay hydrated to avoid altitude sickness.

- **Local Health Services**: Boise has several hospitals and urgent care centers if you need medical assistance during your visit. St. Luke's Boise Medical Center is one of the largest and most trusted facilities in the area.

6. MONEY MATTERS

- **Currency**: The U.S. dollar (USD) is the local currency. Credit and debit cards are widely accepted, but it's a good idea to carry some cash for small purchases or tips.

- **Tipping**: Tipping is customary in Boise, just as in the rest of the U.S. Standard tips include 15-20% at restaurants, $1-2 per bag for hotel bellhops, and $2-5 per day for housekeeping.

- **ATMs**: ATMs are plentiful in Boise, and you'll find them at banks, convenience stores, and shopping centers.

7. LOCAL ETIQUETTE

- **Friendly Locals**: Boiseans are known for their friendliness and hospitality. Don't hesitate to ask for directions or recommendations; locals are usually happy to help.

- **Respect Nature**: Boise's residents take pride in their city's natural beauty. Be sure to follow Leave No Trace principles when enjoying outdoor spaces—dispose of trash properly, stay on designated trails, and respect wildlife.

- **Noise Levels**: Boise is generally a laid-back city, so try to keep noise levels down in public places, especially in residential areas.

8. DINING AND DRINKING

- **Farm-to-Table**: Boise has a growing farm-to-table dining scene. Try to dine at local restaurants that feature Idaho-grown produce and meats.

- **Craft Beer**: Boise boasts a thriving craft beer scene. Visit local breweries like Payette Brewing Co. or Boise Brewing for a taste of Idaho's finest brews.

- **Reservations**: Popular restaurants can get busy, especially on weekends. It's a good idea to make reservations in advance.

9. CULTURAL TIPS

- **Basque Heritage**: Boise has a rich Basque heritage, and you'll find many cultural sites, restaurants, and festivals celebrating this unique part of the city's history. The Basque Block is a must-visit for a taste of Basque culture.

- **Festivals**: Boise hosts several annual festivals, such as Treefort Music Fest and Art in the Park. Check the local event calendar during your visit to experience the city's vibrant cultural scene.

10. COMMUNICATION

- **Language**: English is the primary language spoken in Boise, but you'll also find Spanish speakers and resources available in Spanish.

- **Wi-Fi**: Free Wi-Fi is available in many public places, including cafes, restaurants, and hotels. The Boise Public Library also offers free Wi-Fi.

- **Mobile Service**: Boise has good mobile coverage across all major carriers. If you're traveling from abroad, consider getting a local SIM card or using an international roaming plan.

1.4 FAQS FOR FIRST-TIME VISITORS

If you're planning your first visit to Boise, Idaho, you may have a few questions. Here's a list of frequently asked questions to help you prepare for your trip to the City of Trees.

1. WHAT'S THE BEST TIME OF YEAR TO VISIT BOISE?

Boise is a year-round destination, but the best time to visit depends on your interests:

- **Spring (March to May):** Ideal for mild weather and blooming flowers.

- **Summer (June to August):** Great for outdoor activities, river floats, and festivals.

- **Fall (September to November):** Enjoy cooler temperatures and stunning fall foliage.

- **Winter (December to February):** Perfect for skiing and winter sports at nearby Bogus Basin.

2. HOW DO I GET TO BOISE?

Boise is easily accessible by air, car, or bus:

- **By Air:** Boise Airport (BOI) is the main airport, with flights from major U.S. cities.

- **By Car:** Interstate 84 runs through Boise, making it easy to drive from nearby cities.

- **By Bus:** Greyhound and other bus services connect Boise with surrounding regions.

3. DO I NEED A VISA TO VISIT BOISE?

- **U.S. Citizens:** No visa is required for U.S. citizens.

- **International Visitors:** Depending on your country of origin, you may need a U.S. visa. Check the U.S. Department of State's website for specific visa requirements.

4. WHAT'S THE BEST WAY TO GET AROUND BOISE?

- **Walking:** Downtown Boise is very walkable, with most attractions within easy reach.

- **Biking:** Boise is bike-friendly, and you can rent bikes from local shops or use Boise GreenBike.

- **Public Transit:** ValleyRide offers bus services throughout Boise and nearby areas.

- **Ride-Sharing:** Uber and Lyft are widely available.

5. WHAT SHOULD I PACK FOR MY TRIP TO BOISE?

- **Clothing Layers:** Boise's weather can vary, so pack layers for flexibility.

- **Comfortable Shoes:** Essential for exploring the city and outdoor trails.

- **Sun Protection:** Sunscreen, sunglasses, and a hat are recommended, especially in summer.

- **Reusable Water Bottle:** Handy for staying hydrated during outdoor activities.

6. WHAT ARE THE MUST-SEE ATTRACTIONS IN BOISE?

Some of Boise's top attractions include:

- **Boise River Greenbelt:** A scenic 25-mile path along the Boise River.

- **Old Idaho Penitentiary:** A historic site offering tours and exhibits.

- **Boise Art Museum:** Showcasing contemporary and regional art.

- **Idaho State Capitol:** A beautiful and historic government building.

- **Julia Davis Park:** A large park with museums, gardens, and a zoo.

7. IS BOISE A GOOD DESTINATION FOR OUTDOOR ACTIVITIES?

Absolutely! Boise is an outdoor enthusiast's paradise with activities like:

- **Hiking:** Explore the Boise Foothills and numerous nearby trails.

- **Biking:** Bike along the Greenbelt or hit the mountain trails.

- **Skiing:** Bogus Basin offers great skiing and snowboarding in winter.

- **River Activities:** Enjoy fishing, kayaking, or floating on the Boise River.

8. WHAT ARE THE BEST PLACES TO EAT IN BOISE?

Boise has a thriving food scene with options for every palate:

- **Downtown:** Try farm-to-table restaurants, Basque cuisine, and craft breweries.

- **The North End:** Known for its eclectic eateries and cafes.

- **Capital City Public Market:** Great for sampling local produce and artisanal foods.

9. IS BOISE A SAFE CITY TO VISIT?

Boise is considered a very safe city with friendly locals. Like any city, it's wise to stay aware of your surroundings, especially at night, but overall, Boise offers a welcoming and secure environment for visitors.

10. CAN I VISIT BOISE ON A BUDGET?

Yes, Boise is a budget-friendly destination with many free or low-cost activities:

- **Parks and Greenbelt:** Free to explore and enjoy.

- **Free Attractions:** Visit the Idaho State Capitol or take a self-guided walking tour of the city's murals and public art.

- **Affordable Dining:** Boise offers a range of dining options, from food trucks to casual eateries, that won't break the bank.

11. DO I NEED A CAR IN BOISE?

While having a car is convenient for exploring the surrounding areas, it's not necessary for getting around downtown Boise. The city's public transportation, bike rentals, and walkable streets make it easy to explore without a car.

12. WHAT LOCAL CUSTOMS OR ETIQUETTE SHOULD I BE AWARE OF?

- **Friendly Locals:** Boiseans are known for their hospitality. Don't hesitate to greet people or ask for help.

- **Respect Nature:** Boise takes pride in its natural beauty, so be sure to follow Leave No Trace principles when enjoying outdoor spaces.

- **Tipping:** It's customary to tip 15-20% at restaurants and a few dollars for hotel staff or taxi drivers.

13. WHERE CAN I STAY IN BOISE?

Boise offers a variety of accommodations to suit different preferences and budgets:

- **Downtown Hotels:** Close to major attractions, dining, and nightlife.

- **Boutique Hotels:** Unique and charming options in the heart of the city.

- **Budget-Friendly:** Several motels and chain hotels offer affordable rates.

- **Vacation Rentals:** Options include apartments, homes, and cabins, often with more space and amenities.

14. *WHAT EVENTS OR FESTIVALS SHOULD I ATTEND IN BOISE?*

Boise hosts several annual events that are worth checking out:

- **Treefort Music Fest:** A popular multi-day music festival held every March.

- **Art in the Park:** An outdoor arts and crafts festival in September.

- **Boise Farmers Market:** Held weekly from April to December, offering local produce and goods.

15. *HOW DO I CONNECT TO THE INTERNET IN BOISE?*

- **Wi-Fi:** Free Wi-Fi is available in many public places, including cafes, restaurants, and hotels.

- **Mobile Service:** Boise has good mobile coverage from all major carriers. If you're traveling internationally, consider getting a local SIM card or using an international roaming plan.

CHAPTER 2: BOISE AT A GLANCE

2.1 OVERVIEW OF THE CITY

Boise, the capital city of Idaho, is a vibrant, welcoming, and dynamic destination that beautifully balances urban sophistication with natural charm. Nestled in the Treasure Valley and surrounded by the picturesque Boise Foothills, this city offers a perfect blend of outdoor adventure, rich history, and modern culture, making it a must-visit for travelers from all walks of life.

THE CITY OF TREES

Boise is affectionately known as the "City of Trees," a nickname that speaks to the city's lush, green environment. This moniker originated in the 1800s when early settlers marveled at the dense forests along the Boise River. Today, this connection to nature remains strong, with tree-lined streets, expansive parks, and the 25-mile-long Boise River Greenbelt that winds through the heart of the city, providing a scenic and serene escape for residents and visitors alike.

A GATEWAY TO ADVENTURE

Boise's location makes it an ideal gateway to a wide range of outdoor activities. The Boise Foothills, with their extensive network of trails, offer hiking, mountain biking, and breathtaking views of the city and beyond. Just a short drive away, Bogus Basin Mountain Recreation Area provides year-round activities, from skiing and snowboarding in the winter to mountain biking and scenic chairlift rides in the summer. For water enthusiasts, the Boise River is perfect for fishing, kayaking, or simply floating lazily on a summer day.

A THRIVING CULTURAL SCENE

While Boise is deeply connected to its natural surroundings, it also boasts a thriving cultural scene. The city is home to a vibrant arts community, with numerous galleries, theaters, and live music venues that showcase local talent and international acts. The Boise Art Museum, with its impressive collection of contemporary and regional art, is a cultural gem, while the Morrison Center for the Performing Arts hosts everything from Broadway shows to symphony performances.

Boise's Basque heritage is another unique cultural aspect of the city. The Basque Block, located in downtown Boise, is a hub of Basque culture in the United States, featuring traditional restaurants, cultural centers, and festivals that celebrate this rich heritage.

HISTORY AND HERITAGE

Boise's history is as rich as its culture. The city was founded in 1863 during the gold rush and quickly grew as a trade center for miners and settlers. Today, visitors can explore this history through landmarks like the Old

Idaho Penitentiary, a preserved prison with exhibits that offer a glimpse into Idaho's past, or the Idaho State Capitol, an architectural masterpiece that stands as a symbol of the state's governance and history.

The Basque Museum and Cultural Center and the Idaho State Historical Museum also offer deep dives into the region's past, providing context and stories that help visitors understand the city's unique identity.

A CULINARY DESTINATION

Boise's culinary scene is a delightful surprise for many visitors. The city has embraced the farm-to-table movement, with many restaurants focusing on fresh, locally sourced ingredients. From fine dining establishments to casual eateries, Boise offers a range of dining experiences that cater to every palate. The city is also known for its burgeoning craft beer scene, with numerous breweries offering unique and flavorful brews that reflect Idaho's agricultural bounty.

The Capital City Public Market, held weekly in downtown Boise, is a highlight for food lovers, offering a wide array of local produce, artisanal products, and gourmet treats.

A WELCOMING COMMUNITY

One of the first things you'll notice about Boise is its warm, welcoming atmosphere. The city's residents, known as Boiseans, are friendly and hospitable, often going out of their way to make visitors feel at home. This strong sense of community is evident in the city's numerous festivals, farmers' markets, and public events, where locals and visitors alike come together to celebrate the city's vibrant culture.

Boise's neighborhoods each have their own unique charm, from the historic North End with its beautifully preserved homes and tree-lined streets to the bustling downtown area, where you'll find an eclectic mix of shops, cafes, and cultural attractions.

A HUB FOR INNOVATION AND EDUCATION

Boise is not just a great place to visit; it's also a thriving hub for business, innovation, and education. The city is home to several major companies, including Micron Technology and Albertsons, and has a growing tech scene that attracts entrepreneurs and startups. Boise State University, with its iconic blue football field, is a central part of the community, contributing to the city's youthful energy and providing a strong educational foundation.

BOISE'S CLIMATE

Boise enjoys a semi-arid climate, characterized by four distinct seasons. Summers are warm and dry, perfect for outdoor activities, while winters bring snow to the nearby mountains, offering excellent conditions for skiing and snowboarding. Spring and fall are mild, with beautiful foliage and ideal weather for exploring the city's parks and trails.

2.2 HISTORY AND CULTURAL HERITAGE

From its roots as a fort during the gold rush era to its status today as a vibrant cultural hub, Boise's story is one of resilience, diversity, and a deep connection to both the land and its people. Here's a closer look at the history and cultural heritage that define Boise.

EARLY BEGINNINGS: THE FOUNDING OF BOISE

Boise's history dates back to the mid-19th century, during a time of great expansion and exploration in the American West. The area that is now Boise was originally inhabited by the Shoshone-Bannock and Northern Paiute tribes, who lived off the land and maintained a deep connection with the region's natural resources.

The city itself was officially founded in 1863, during the height of the gold rush. Fort Boise was established by the U.S. Army as a military outpost to protect travelers and settlers on the Oregon Trail, as well as to maintain peace with the Native American tribes. The fort was strategically located near the Boise River, providing access to water and serving as a key stopover for pioneers heading west.

The name "Boise" is believed to have originated from the French word "boisé," meaning "wooded," as early French-Canadian fur trappers referred to the area's lush tree-lined riverbanks. As word spread of the fort's establishment, a small town quickly grew around it, becoming a center of trade and commerce for miners and settlers in the region.

THE GOLD RUSH AND GROWTH

Boise's early growth was fueled by the discovery of gold in the nearby Boise Basin, one of the richest gold strikes in American history. Thousands of prospectors flocked to the area in search of fortune, and Boise quickly became a bustling supply center for mining operations. The influx of settlers led to the construction of homes, businesses, and infrastructure, transforming Boise from a small fort town into a thriving community.

In 1864, just a year after its founding, Boise was designated the capital of the Idaho Territory, a status it would retain when Idaho became a state in 1890. The city's role as the territorial and state capital brought a sense of permanence and importance, further driving its growth and development.

BOISE'S BASQUE HERITAGE

One of the most unique aspects of Boise's cultural heritage is its strong Basque influence. Starting in the late 19th century, many Basques emigrated from the Pyrenees region of Spain and France to the United States, with a significant number settling in Boise. They were drawn by the opportunities for work, particularly in sheepherding, which was a common occupation among the Basques.

Today, Boise is home to one of the largest Basque communities in the United States. The Basque Block, located in downtown Boise, is the heart of this vibrant community. Here, visitors can explore the Basque Museum and Cultural Center, which offers insights into Basque history, culture, and contributions to the region. The area is also home to traditional Basque restaurants, a Basque market, and the Basque Center, where cultural events and social gatherings are held.

The annual San Inazio Festival and Jaialdi, a major Basque festival held every five years, celebrate Basque culture with traditional music, dance, sports, and cuisine. These events attract visitors from around the world and are a testament to the enduring legacy of the Basque people in Boise.

THE OLD IDAHO PENITENTIARY

One of Boise's most significant historical landmarks is the Old Idaho Penitentiary, which operated as a prison from 1872 to 1973. Built from local sandstone by the prisoners themselves, the penitentiary housed some of Idaho's most notorious criminals over its 101-year history. Today, the site is a museum that offers visitors a glimpse into the harsh realities of life behind bars in the Old West.

The Old Idaho Penitentiary features several historic buildings, including cell blocks, solitary confinement, the gallows, and the Women's Ward. Exhibits detail the stories of the prisoners who lived and died there, as well as the history of crime and punishment in Idaho. The site is a haunting reminder of the past and a fascinating place for those interested in history.

THE IDAHO STATE CAPITOL

The Idaho State Capitol is another iconic symbol of Boise's history and heritage. Completed in 1920, the Capitol building is an architectural masterpiece constructed from sandstone and marble. It features a grand dome, inspired by the U.S. Capitol, that rises 208 feet above the city.

Inside, the Capitol is filled with historical artifacts, artwork, and exhibits that tell the story of Idaho's journey from a territory to statehood. Visitors can explore the legislative chambers, the Governor's Office, and the beautifully restored rotunda. The Capitol is not only a functioning seat of government but also a place where the public can engage with Idaho's political history.

THE BOISE RIVER GREENBELT

While the Boise River Greenbelt is primarily known as a recreational area, it also has historical significance. The Greenbelt follows the path of the Boise River, which has been a vital resource for the city since its founding. In the late 1960s, efforts were made to preserve the riverfront as a natural space, leading to the development of the Greenbelt, which now spans 25 miles.

The Greenbelt is dotted with historical markers and points of interest, including the site of the original Fort Boise. It's a place where residents and visitors can connect with both nature and the history of the city, all while enjoying the beautiful scenery.

PRESERVING THE PAST: MUSEUMS AND CULTURAL CENTERS

Boise is home to several museums and cultural centers that play a crucial role in preserving and sharing the city's history and heritage. The Idaho State Museum offers a comprehensive look at the state's history, from its Native American roots to its modern-day achievements. The museum's interactive exhibits and artifacts provide a rich, educational experience for visitors of all ages.

The Basque Museum and Cultural Center, as mentioned earlier, is dedicated to preserving the history and culture of the Basque community in Boise. It's a place where visitors can learn about the Basques' contributions to the region and experience their traditions firsthand.

Other cultural institutions, such as the Boise Art Museum and the Boise Philharmonic, contribute to the city's vibrant arts scene, offering exhibitions, performances, and educational programs that celebrate both local and global cultures.

A LEGACY OF COMMUNITY AND PROGRESS

Throughout its history, Boise has been shaped by the diverse communities that have called it home. From the Native American tribes who first inhabited the area to the Basque immigrants who brought their unique culture to the city, Boise's heritage is a tapestry of different cultures, traditions, and stories.

Today, Boise continues to honor its past while embracing progress and innovation. The city's thriving tech sector, growing population, and commitment to sustainability reflect its forward-looking spirit. At the same time, Boiseans remain deeply connected to their history, as seen in the preservation of historic sites, the celebration of cultural festivals, and the community's pride in its heritage.

2.3 LOCAL TRADITIONS AND FESTIVALS

hroughout the year, the city comes alive with vibrant celebrations that showcase its unique blend of cultures, arts, and community spirit. Here's an overview of some of the most cherished local traditions and festivals in Boise.

1. JAIALDI: BOISE'S BASQUE FESTIVAL

One of the most significant cultural events in Boise is **Jaialdi**, an internationally renowned Basque festival held every five years. This celebration of Basque culture is one of the largest in the world, drawing thousands of visitors from across the globe. Jaialdi, which means "festival" in Basque, showcases traditional Basque music, dance, sports, food, and crafts.

The festival takes place over several days and includes events such as Basque dancing performances, exhibitions of Basque rural sports (like wood chopping and stone lifting), and large community picnics. The Basque Block in downtown Boise serves as the heart of the festivities, but events are held throughout the city. Jaialdi is a powerful expression of Boise's deep Basque heritage and offers a unique cultural experience for all who attend.

2. TREEFORT MUSIC FEST

Treefort Music Fest is one of Boise's most popular and rapidly growing festivals, held annually in late March. Since its inception in 2012, Treefort has evolved into a five-day celebration of music, art, film, food, and technology. What started as a music festival has expanded to include multiple "forts," each dedicated to different aspects of culture and creativity.

The festival features hundreds of performances from local, national, and international artists across various genres, with stages set up in venues throughout downtown Boise. In addition to music, attendees can explore other "forts" such as Storyfort (literature and storytelling), Alefort (craft beer), Hackfort (technology and innovation), and Filmfort (independent films).

Treefort's inclusive and community-focused vibe makes it a beloved event for Boise residents and visitors alike. It's a celebration of the city's creativity and a showcase of its vibrant arts scene.

3. BOISE PRIDE FESTIVAL

The **Boise Pride Festival** is a major annual event that celebrates the LGBTQ+ community in Boise and promotes inclusivity, diversity, and equality. Held every June during Pride Month, the festival features a colorful parade through downtown Boise, live music performances, drag shows, and a wide range of vendors and informational booths.

Boise Pride is a family-friendly event that attracts thousands of participants and spectators, making it one of the largest LGBTQ+ events in Idaho. The festival is a testament to Boise's commitment to fostering an inclusive and welcoming environment for all residents and visitors.

4. ART IN THE PARK

Every September, Boise's **Art in the Park** transforms Julia Davis Park into a vibrant outdoor gallery. Organized by the Boise Art Museum, this three-day event is one of the largest and most popular art festivals in the region. Art in the Park features more than 200 artists and vendors from across the country, showcasing a wide variety of handmade art, including paintings, sculptures, ceramics, jewelry, and textiles.

In addition to the art displays, the festival offers live music, food vendors, and hands-on activities for children. Art in the Park is a cherished tradition in Boise, attracting art enthusiasts and families for a weekend of creativity and community.

5. BOISE FARMERS MARKET

The **Boise Farmers Market** is a beloved weekly tradition that runs from April through December. Held every Saturday morning, the market is a gathering place for locals and visitors to enjoy fresh, locally grown produce, artisanal foods, and handmade crafts.

The market features a wide variety of vendors offering everything from organic vegetables and fruits to fresh-baked goods, cheeses, meats, and flowers. It's also a great place to sample local specialties, discover unique products, and meet the farmers and artisans behind them. The Boise Farmers Market is not just about shopping; it's a social event where the community comes together to support local agriculture and sustainable practices.

6. SAN INAZIO FESTIVAL

The **San Inazio Festival** is another important celebration of Boise's Basque heritage, held annually at the end of July. Named after St. Ignatius of Loyola, the patron saint of the Basques, this festival is a weekend-long event that includes traditional Basque dancing, music, sports, and a large community picnic.

The San Inazio Festival is centered around the Basque Block, where participants can enjoy authentic Basque food, watch pelota (a traditional Basque sport), and listen to performances by Basque musicians. The festival is a key event for Boise's Basque community and offers a chance for visitors to experience the warmth and vibrancy of Basque culture.

7. IDAHO SHAKESPEARE FESTIVAL

The **Idaho Shakespeare Festival** is a long-standing tradition in Boise, offering high-quality theatrical performances in a beautiful outdoor setting. The festival runs from May through September at the stunning amphitheater located along the Boise River, surrounded by natural landscapes.

The festival's repertoire includes classic Shakespearean plays, contemporary dramas, and comedies, all performed by talented actors and directors. The outdoor setting adds a magical element to the performances, making it a popular summer activity for both locals and visitors. Audiences are encouraged to bring picnic baskets and enjoy a leisurely evening of theater under the stars.

8. SPIRIT OF BOISE BALLOON CLASSIC

The **Spirit of Boise Balloon Classic** is a breathtaking event that fills the Boise sky with a colorful array of hot air balloons every year around Labor Day weekend. This five-day festival is held at Ann Morrison Park and attracts balloonists from across the country.

The event begins with morning launches, where visitors can watch dozens of hot air balloons take flight against the backdrop of the rising sun. One of the highlights of the festival is the Night Glow event, where the balloons are tethered and illuminated, creating a magical display of light and color. The Spirit of Boise Balloon Classic is a family-friendly event that offers a unique and awe-inspiring experience.

9. WINTER GARDEN AGLOW

During the holiday season, the Idaho Botanical Garden transforms into a winter wonderland for the **Winter Garden aGlow** event. From late November through December, the garden is adorned with over 500,000 sparkling lights, creating a festive and enchanting atmosphere.

Visitors can stroll through the illuminated gardens, enjoy hot cocoa, and visit Santa Claus. The event also features holiday music, live performances, and activities for children. Winter Garden aGlow is a cherished holiday tradition in Boise, bringing joy and warmth to all who attend.

10. EAGLE ISLAND EXPERIENCE

The **Eagle Island Experience** is a summer festival held at Eagle Island State Park, just a short drive from Boise. This family-friendly event celebrates the natural beauty and outdoor recreation opportunities of the area with activities such as paddleboarding, kayaking, and zip-lining.

The festival also features live music, food trucks, and local vendors, making it a fun and relaxing way to spend a summer day. The Eagle Island Experience is a testament to Boise's love of the outdoors and its commitment to providing accessible recreational activities for all.

2.4 MUST-KNOW LOCAL ETIQUETTE

When visiting Boise, understanding and respecting the local customs and etiquette can enhance your experience and help you connect with the community. Boise is known for its friendly and welcoming atmosphere, but like any place, there are certain norms and expectations that visitors should be aware of. Here's a guide to the must-know local etiquette in Boise.

1. FRIENDLY GREETINGS AND INTERACTIONS

- **Say Hello**: Boiseans are known for their friendliness. It's common to greet people with a smile, a nod, or a simple "hello," whether you're passing them on a hiking trail, in a park, or on the street. Don't be surprised if strangers strike up a conversation—it's all part of the local charm.

- **Politeness Matters**: Being polite and respectful in your interactions is highly valued in Boise. Simple courtesies like saying "please," "thank you," and "excuse me" go a long way in making a positive impression.

2. RESPECT FOR NATURE

- **Leave No Trace**: Boiseans take great pride in their natural surroundings, and there's a strong emphasis on environmental stewardship. When enjoying the city's parks, trails, and outdoor spaces, be sure to follow the Leave No Trace principles. This means packing out all trash, staying on designated trails, and not disturbing wildlife.

- **Keep It Clean**: Whether you're picnicking in a park or floating down the Boise River, always clean up after yourself. Littering is frowned upon, and maintaining the cleanliness of public spaces is a shared responsibility.

3. TRAFFIC AND PEDESTRIAN ETIQUETTE

- **Yield to Pedestrians**: Boise is a pedestrian-friendly city, and drivers are expected to yield to pedestrians at crosswalks. As a pedestrian, it's important to use crosswalks and wait for the appropriate signals when crossing streets.

- **Share the Greenbelt**: The Boise River Greenbelt is a popular spot for walking, running, and biking. When using the Greenbelt, stay to the right to allow others to pass, and give a friendly verbal warning (like "on your left") when overtaking someone. Be mindful of your speed, especially in crowded areas, and always be courteous to other users.

4. DINING OUT

- **Tipping**: Tipping is customary in Boise, just as it is throughout the United States. A standard tip of 15-20% of the total bill is expected in restaurants. For exceptional service, consider tipping even more. Don't forget to tip bartenders, baristas, and other service workers as well.

- **Local and Sustainable Choices**: Boise has a strong farm-to-table movement, and many locals prefer dining at establishments that source ingredients locally and sustainably. When in Boise, consider supporting these businesses by choosing locally owned restaurants and trying dishes made with Idaho-grown produce and meats.

5. PUBLIC SPACES AND NOISE LEVELS

- **Keep Noise Levels Down**: Boise is generally a quiet and peaceful city, especially in residential neighborhoods and public parks. It's important to keep noise levels down, particularly in the evening and early morning hours. When enjoying the outdoors, be mindful of others who may be seeking peace and quiet.

- **Respect Personal Space**: Boiseans appreciate their personal space, especially in public settings. When standing in line, sitting on public transportation, or walking on crowded streets, it's courteous to give others enough room.

6. OUTDOOR ETIQUETTE

- **Be Prepared for the Outdoors**: Boise's natural beauty is one of its biggest attractions, but it's important to be prepared when exploring the outdoors. Bring plenty of water, wear appropriate footwear, and be aware of the weather conditions. Boiseans value self-reliance, so being well-prepared shows respect for both the environment and your fellow adventurers.

- **Respect Wildlife**: If you encounter wildlife while hiking or exploring, observe from a distance and avoid feeding animals. This helps protect both you and the animals, and it preserves the natural behavior of wildlife.

7. CULTURAL RESPECT

- **Honor Local Traditions**: Boise has a rich cultural heritage, including a significant Basque community. When attending cultural events or visiting cultural sites, it's important to show respect for the traditions and practices you encounter. Participate with an open mind, and don't hesitate to ask questions if you're unsure about something.

- **Support Local Art and Music**: Boise has a thriving arts scene, and locals take pride in supporting their artists and musicians. When visiting galleries, attending performances, or exploring local markets, show your appreciation for the creativity and talent on display by supporting local artists and performers.

8. PARTICIPATION IN COMMUNITY EVENTS

- **Join In**: Boise is a community-oriented city, and visitors are often welcomed to participate in local events, festivals, and gatherings. Whether it's a farmers market, a neighborhood block party, or a cultural festival, don't hesitate to join in and engage with the community.

- **Volunteer**: Volunteering is a big part of Boise's community spirit. If you're staying in the city for an extended period, consider volunteering for local causes or events. It's a great way to meet people and give back to the community.

9. HEALTH AND SAFETY CONSIDERATIONS

- **Respect for COVID-19 Guidelines**: Like many places, Boise has had to adapt to the ongoing challenges of the COVID-19 pandemic. Be sure to follow any local health guidelines, such as wearing masks in certain settings, maintaining social distancing, and using hand sanitizer. Boiseans value the health and safety of their community, and respecting these guidelines is appreciated.

- **Emergency Services**: In case of an emergency, Boise's emergency services are highly responsive. Dial 911 for emergencies, and be aware of the locations of nearby hospitals and urgent care centers.

CHAPTER 3: EXPLORING DOWNTOWN BOISE

3.1 BOISE RIVER GREENBELT: PARKS AND PATHWAYS

This 25-mile-long pathway meanders alongside the Boise River, connecting a series of parks, natural areas, and vibrant neighborhoods. Whether you're looking to take a leisurely stroll, go for a bike ride, or simply enjoy the natural beauty of the area, the Greenbelt is an ideal destination for both locals and visitors. Here's a guide to the parks and pathways that make the Boise River Greenbelt a must-visit during your stay in Boise.

1. ANN MORRISON PARK

Ann Morrison Park is one of the largest and most popular parks along the Boise River Greenbelt. Spanning over 150 acres, this expansive green space offers a wide range of recreational activities and amenities. The park features open fields, playgrounds, picnic areas, and sports facilities, including tennis courts, a disc golf course, and a softball complex.

One of the park's highlights is the Boise River's Lazy River, a gentle waterway where visitors can enjoy floating on a warm summer day. Ann Morrison Park also hosts various events and festivals throughout the year, making it a lively and dynamic part of the Greenbelt.

- **Must-See Spot:** The fountain and rose garden, located near the center of the park, offer a peaceful retreat and a perfect spot for photos.

2. JULIA DAVIS PARK

Just a short walk from downtown Boise, Julia Davis Park is a cultural and recreational hub within the Greenbelt. Established in 1907, it is Boise's oldest park and is home to several of the city's most notable attractions, including the Boise Art Museum, Zoo Boise, the Idaho State Museum, and the Discovery Center of Idaho.

The park itself is a beautiful space with shady trees, rose gardens, and picnic areas, making it a popular spot for families and visitors looking to relax and enjoy the outdoors. The park's scenic pond, complete with paddleboats for rent, adds to its charm.

- **Must-See Spot:** The Friendship Bridge, a pedestrian bridge that connects Julia Davis Park to Boise State University, offers stunning views of the river and is a favorite spot for photos.

3. KATHRYN ALBERTSON PARK

Kathryn Albertson Park is a hidden gem along the Boise River Greenbelt, known for its tranquil atmosphere and natural beauty. This 41-acre park is designed as a wildlife sanctuary, with carefully landscaped ponds, meadows, and wetlands that attract a variety of birds and other wildlife.

The park's winding pathways and peaceful settings make it a perfect place for a leisurely walk or quiet reflection. Interpretive signs along the paths provide information about the park's flora and fauna, adding an educational element to your visit.

- **Must-See Spot:** The gazebo at the park's central pond is a serene location to sit and watch the ducks and other wildlife that frequent the area.

4. VETERANS MEMORIAL PARK

Located on the northern edge of the Greenbelt, Veterans Memorial Park is a peaceful tribute to the men and women who have served in the military. The park features a large open lawn, a memorial plaza with monuments, and shaded picnic areas. It's a quiet spot for reflection and a great starting point for exploring the Greenbelt's northern sections.

The park also provides access to the riparian areas along the Boise River, where you can enjoy birdwatching or fishing. It's a lovely area to explore if you're looking for a more contemplative experience along the Greenbelt.

- **Must-See Spot:** The Veterans Memorial Plaza, which includes a series of monuments and plaques dedicated to veterans, offers a solemn and respectful atmosphere.

5. BERNARDINE QUINN RIVERSIDE PARK

Bernardine Quinn Riverside Park is one of the newer additions to the Boise River Greenbelt. This park is best known for Quinn's Pond, a large, calm body of water that's perfect for water sports. Visitors can rent paddleboards, kayaks, and canoes from local outfitters and spend the day exploring the pond or relaxing on its shores.

The park also features sandy beaches, picnic areas, and access to the Whitewater Park, where adventurous visitors can try their hand at kayaking or surfing on the engineered waves.

- **Must-See Spot:** Quinn's Pond is the centerpiece of the park and offers a beautiful setting for both active and relaxing outdoor activities.

6. ESTHER SIMPLOT PARK

Directly adjacent to Quinn's Pond is Esther Simplot Park, a 55-acre oasis that's a favorite among Boise residents. This park features a series of interconnected ponds, wetlands, and pathways that create a natural and serene environment. It's a great spot for walking, birdwatching, or simply enjoying the water views.

Esther Simplot Park is also home to a popular playground, picnic shelters, and a sandy beach area, making it a family-friendly destination along the Greenbelt.

- **Must-See Spot:** The sand volleyball courts near the park's main pond are a popular spot for both casual and competitive games, adding to the park's lively atmosphere.

7. MUNICIPAL PARK

Municipal Park is another beloved park along the Greenbelt, known for its large shady trees and tranquil setting. The park features picnic areas, playgrounds, and open spaces perfect for a game of frisbee or a leisurely afternoon. The Morrison Knudsen Nature Center, located within the park, offers educational exhibits and wildlife viewing areas, including a trout stream and a pond with a variety of native fish species.

The park's proximity to the Greenbelt makes it an excellent starting point for a bike ride or walk along the river, and it's a favorite spot for family gatherings and outdoor events.

- **Must-See Spot:** The Morrison Knudsen Nature Center, with its underwater viewing windows and educational displays, is a must-visit for nature enthusiasts of all ages.

8. BOISE WHITEWATER PARK

Boise Whitewater Park is a unique feature of the Greenbelt that caters to adventure seekers and water sports enthusiasts. This engineered section of the Boise River offers adjustable waves and rapids that attract kayakers, surfers, and paddleboarders from across the region. Whether you're participating or simply watching from the riverbank, the Whitewater Park adds a thrilling dimension to the Greenbelt experience.

The park is also connected to the nearby Esther Simplot and Quinn's Pond parks, making it easy to combine a visit to the Whitewater Park with other outdoor activities.

- **Must-See Spot:** The viewing platform along the river offers a great vantage point to watch the skilled kayakers and surfers navigate the waves.

3.2 BOISE ART MUSEUM AND CULTURAL DISTRICT

The Boise Art Museum (BAM) and the surrounding Cultural District are at the heart of Boise's vibrant arts and cultural scene. This area is a must-visit for anyone interested in exploring the city's rich artistic heritage, contemporary creativity, and cultural offerings. Here's an overview of what you can expect when you dive into the Boise Art Museum and the Cultural District.

BOISE ART MUSEUM (BAM)

1. Overview

The Boise Art Museum, commonly known as BAM, is one of the city's premier cultural institutions. Established in 1937, BAM has grown from a small local gallery into a leading museum with a diverse and dynamic collection of art from around the world. Located in Julia Davis Park, BAM is a central piece of Boise's Cultural District and offers visitors an inspiring and educational experience.

2. Exhibits and Collections

BAM's permanent collection includes more than 3,500 works of art, with a strong emphasis on contemporary art, regional artists, and works that reflect the cultural diversity of the American West. The museum's collection spans various mediums, including painting, sculpture, photography, ceramics, and mixed media.

In addition to its permanent collection, BAM hosts rotating exhibitions that feature works from renowned artists, traveling exhibits, and thematic displays that offer fresh perspectives on art and culture. Past exhibitions have included everything from Native American art to modern photography, ensuring there's always something new and exciting to discover.

3. Special Programs and Events

BAM is more than just a museum—it's a community hub for art education and engagement. The museum offers a wide range of programs and events designed to connect visitors of all ages with the world of art. These include:

- **Art Talks and Lectures:** Engage with curators, artists, and scholars through insightful talks and discussions about current exhibits and broader art topics.

- **Workshops and Classes:** BAM offers hands-on art workshops and classes for both children and adults, providing opportunities to learn new skills and explore creative expression.

- **Family Days:** Special events designed for families, offering interactive activities, art-making stations, and guided tours tailored for younger audiences.

- **Annual Art in the Park:** BAM's largest fundraiser, this outdoor art festival held every September in Julia Davis Park, brings together artists and craftspeople from around the country, offering visitors a chance to purchase unique art pieces while supporting the museum.

4. Architecture and Space

BAM's building itself is a work of art. The museum underwent a significant expansion and renovation in the late 1990s, which added contemporary design elements and expanded gallery space. The building's architecture is designed to create an inviting and contemplative environment, with natural light filtering through large windows, spacious galleries, and outdoor sculpture gardens that seamlessly blend with the park's natural beauty.

5. Museum Shop and Café

Before you leave BAM, be sure to stop by the museum shop, which offers a curated selection of art books, unique gifts, and locally made crafts. The shop is a great place to find a special souvenir or a gift for an art lover.

While BAM doesn't have an on-site café, the museum is conveniently located near several dining options in the Cultural District, where you can enjoy a meal or a coffee after your visit.

THE CULTURAL DISTRICT

1. Overview

The Cultural District surrounding the Boise Art Museum is a vibrant area that's home to a variety of cultural institutions, galleries, theaters, and public art installations. This district is the epicenter of Boise's creative community, offering a rich array of experiences that celebrate the arts, history, and cultural diversity.

2. Key Attractions in the Cultural District

- **Julia Davis Park:** BAM is situated within Julia Davis Park, which is also home to several other cultural institutions, including the Idaho State Museum, Zoo Boise, and the Discovery Center of Idaho. The park itself is a beautiful green space perfect for a leisurely stroll, a picnic, or simply enjoying the outdoor sculptures and river views.

- **Idaho State Museum:** Located just a short walk from BAM, the Idaho State Museum offers a comprehensive look at the state's history, from its Native American roots to its contemporary culture. Interactive exhibits, artifacts, and multimedia presentations make this museum a great complement to your visit to BAM.

- **The Basque Block:** A short distance from the Cultural District, the Basque Block is a unique area dedicated to Boise's rich Basque heritage. Here, you can explore the Basque Museum and Cultural Center, dine on traditional Basque cuisine, and experience the vibrant culture of one of Boise's most distinctive communities.

- **The Morrison Center for the Performing Arts:** Located on the nearby Boise State University campus, the Morrison Center is Boise's premier venue for live performances. The center hosts a wide range of events, including Broadway shows, concerts, ballets, and more. It's a must-visit for performing arts enthusiasts.

- **Freak Alley Gallery:** An open-air mural gallery located in the heart of downtown Boise, Freak Alley is a vibrant display of street art and graffiti. The gallery is free to visit and features ever-changing works by local and international artists, making it a dynamic and colorful addition to the Cultural District.

3. Public Art and Murals

The Cultural District is also known for its impressive public art installations and murals that add a creative flair to the city's streetscapes. As you explore the district, keep an eye out for these artistic expressions that celebrate Boise's cultural diversity and artistic talent.

- **Downtown Boise Murals:** Throughout the Cultural District and downtown area, you'll find a variety of large-scale murals depicting everything from Idaho's natural beauty to abstract designs and social commentary. These murals are a testament to Boise's thriving arts scene and are popular spots for photos.

- **Sculpture Installations:** In addition to murals, the district features several public sculptures, many of which are located in or near Julia Davis Park. These installations range from traditional statues to contemporary works, offering something for every art lover to appreciate.

4. Dining and Shopping in the Cultural District

The Cultural District is not only a haven for art and culture but also a great place to explore Boise's culinary and shopping scenes. The area boasts a variety of dining options, from upscale restaurants to casual cafes, many of which emphasize locally sourced ingredients and creative menus.

For shopping, the district offers a mix of boutique stores, art galleries, and specialty shops where you can find unique gifts, handmade crafts, and locally produced goods. Whether you're looking for a special piece of art, a stylish outfit, or a memorable souvenir, the Cultural District has plenty to offer.

3.3 CAPITOL BUILDING AND HISTORIC LANDMARKS

These sites offer visitors a glimpse into the city's rich past, from its early days as a frontier town to its development as the state's political and cultural center. Whether you're a history enthusiast or simply looking to explore Boise's architectural gems, the Capitol Building and historic landmarks provide a fascinating journey through time.

IDAHO STATE CAPITOL BUILDING

1. Overview

The Idaho State Capitol Building is the crown jewel of Boise's historic landmarks and a symbol of the state's government. Located at the heart of downtown Boise, the Capitol is a stunning example of neoclassical architecture, designed to reflect the ideals of democracy and governance. Completed in 1920, the building is not only a functional seat of the state government but also a historical and architectural treasure.

2. Architecture and Design

The Capitol Building's design is a blend of classical elements, inspired by the U.S. Capitol in Washington, D.C. The exterior is constructed of sandstone and marble, sourced from local quarries, giving the building a distinctive and stately appearance. The most striking feature is the dome, which rises 208 feet above the city and is crowned by a bronze eagle.

Inside, the Capitol is equally impressive, with grand staircases, marble columns, and intricate details throughout. The building's interior features a mix of materials, including marble from Alaska, Georgia, Vermont, and Italy, and the floors are made of beautiful mosaic tile. The rotunda, with its soaring dome and expansive skylight, is the centerpiece of the Capitol and a highlight for visitors.

3. Visiting the Capitol

The Idaho State Capitol is open to the public, and visitors are encouraged to explore its halls and chambers. Self-guided tours are available, allowing you to discover the building at your own pace, or you can join a guided tour for more in-depth information about the history and architecture of the Capitol.

Key areas to explore include:

- **The Rotunda**: The central area beneath the dome, featuring statues, historical displays, and a stunning view of the dome's interior.

- **The Legislative Chambers**: The House and Senate chambers, where Idaho's laws are debated and passed, are open to visitors when the legislature is not in session.

- **The Governor's Office**: While access to the Governor's Office is restricted, visitors can view the office's entrance and learn about Idaho's executive branch.

- **The Statuary and Artworks**: The Capitol is home to numerous statues, portraits, and historical artifacts that tell the story of Idaho's leaders and significant events.

4. Capitol Grounds

The Capitol grounds are beautifully landscaped and feature several monuments and memorials that honor Idaho's history and its citizens' contributions. Notable monuments include the Idaho Liberty Bell, a replica of the Liberty Bell in Philadelphia, and the Idaho Women's Suffrage Memorial, commemorating the state's early adoption of women's suffrage.

The grounds are also a popular spot for civic events, public gatherings, and peaceful reflection, offering a serene setting in the midst of downtown Boise.

HISTORIC LANDMARKS IN BOISE

1. Old Idaho Penitentiary

One of Boise's most fascinating historic sites is the **Old Idaho Penitentiary**, which operated as a prison from 1872 to 1973. Located east of downtown Boise, the penitentiary housed some of the state's most notorious criminals and offers a unique glimpse into Idaho's history of crime and punishment.

Visitors to the Old Idaho Penitentiary can explore the original cell blocks, solitary confinement, the gallows, and the Women's Ward. The site includes several exhibits detailing the history of the prison, infamous inmates, and the harsh conditions of life behind bars. The Old Idaho Penitentiary is also known for its beautiful rose garden, which was originally tended by inmates and continues to bloom today.

- **Don't Miss:** The prison's historic executions and escape attempts are covered in the exhibits, adding to the site's eerie and intriguing atmosphere.

2. Basque Block

The **Basque Block** in downtown Boise is a testament to the city's rich Basque heritage, one of the most significant cultural influences in the region. This area is home to the Basque Museum and Cultural Center, which tells the story of the Basque immigrants who settled in Idaho and their contributions to the state's development.

Visitors to the Basque Block can explore the museum, dine at traditional Basque restaurants, and participate in cultural events such as the San Inazio Festival. The area is also home to the Cyrus Jacobs-Uberuaga House, one of the oldest surviving homes in Boise and a key site in the preservation of Basque history.

- **Don't Miss:** The Basque Block is not just a historic site but also a vibrant community space where you can experience Basque music, dance, and cuisine.

3. Julia Davis Park

Julia Davis Park is one of Boise's oldest and most beloved parks, donated to the city in 1907 by Thomas Jefferson Davis in memory of his wife, Julia. The park is not only a beautiful green space along the Boise River but also home to several important cultural and historic institutions.

In addition to the Boise Art Museum and Zoo Boise, Julia Davis Park houses the Idaho State Museum and the Discovery Center of Idaho. The park's historic Rose Garden, established in 1939, is a popular spot for visitors, featuring a wide variety of rose species and providing a peaceful retreat in the heart of the city.

- **Don't Miss:** The Idaho State Museum offers interactive exhibits and artifacts that provide a comprehensive overview of Idaho's history, making it a perfect complement to your visit to the Capitol Building.

4. Union Pacific Depot

The **Union Pacific Depot**, also known as the Boise Depot, is a historic train station that has been a landmark in Boise since its opening in 1925. Designed in the Spanish Colonial Revival style, the depot is an architectural gem with its iconic tower and beautiful interiors.

The depot no longer serves as a train station, but it has been preserved as a public event space and offers stunning views of downtown Boise and the Boise foothills. The surrounding gardens, known as Platt Gardens, add to the charm of this historic site, making it a popular location for weddings and special events.

- **Don't Miss:** The panoramic view from the depot's bell tower is one of the best in Boise, offering a sweeping vista of the city and the surrounding mountains.

5. St. John's Cathedral

St. John's Cathedral is a historic Roman Catholic cathedral located in downtown Boise. Completed in 1921, the cathedral is a stunning example of Romanesque Revival architecture, with its grand façade, twin towers, and intricate stained glass windows.

The cathedral's interior is equally impressive, featuring beautiful mosaics, a marble altar, and detailed woodwork. St. John's Cathedral is not only a place of worship but also a significant historic and architectural landmark in Boise, welcoming visitors to explore its rich history and spiritual heritage.

- **Don't Miss:** The cathedral's stained glass windows are a highlight, depicting scenes from the Bible and adding to the serene and contemplative atmosphere of the interior.

6. Pioneer Cemetery

Boise's **Pioneer Cemetery** (formerly known as Fort Boise Military Cemetery) is one of the city's oldest cemeteries, dating back to the 1860s. The cemetery is the final resting place for many of Boise's early settlers, pioneers, and military personnel.

Walking through Pioneer Cemetery offers a poignant connection to Boise's past, with historic headstones and monuments that tell the stories of those who helped shape the city. The cemetery is located in the Boise foothills, providing a peaceful and reflective setting.

- **Don't Miss:** The historic gravesites and the unique epitaphs found throughout the cemetery offer insights into the lives and times of Boise's earliest residents.

3.4 8TH STREET: SHOPPING, DINING, AND ENTERTAINMENT

8th Street in downtown Boise is the city's pulse, offering a lively mix of shopping, dining, and entertainment that attracts locals and visitors alike. This vibrant thoroughfare, which stretches through the heart of the city, is a must-visit destination for anyone looking to experience Boise's eclectic urban culture. Whether you're in the mood for a shopping spree, a culinary adventure, or a night out on the town, 8th Street has something for everyone. Here's an overview of what you can expect to find along this bustling street.

SHOPPING ON 8TH STREET

1. Boutique Stores and Specialty Shops

8th Street is home to a variety of boutique stores and specialty shops that offer unique and locally-made goods. Whether you're looking for fashionable clothing, handcrafted jewelry, or artisanal products, you'll find plenty of options to satisfy your shopping cravings.

- **Shift Boutique**: A trendy women's boutique offering a carefully curated selection of stylish clothing, accessories, and gifts. Shift is known for its friendly staff and unique pieces that are perfect for adding a touch of Boise flair to your wardrobe.

- **Idaho Made**: This cooperative shop features handmade products from local artisans, including home décor, jewelry, art, and more. It's an excellent place to pick up one-of-a-kind souvenirs or gifts that showcase Idaho's creative spirit.

- **Mixed Greens**: A delightful store that blends the best of art and home décor, Mixed Greens offers an eclectic mix of locally made crafts, quirky gifts, and eco-friendly products. It's a great spot to find something truly unique for your home or as a gift.

2. Art Galleries and Creative Spaces

In addition to retail stores, 8th Street is dotted with art galleries and creative spaces where you can explore Boise's thriving arts scene.

- **Boise Art Glass**: Located just off 8th Street, Boise Art Glass is a working glass studio where you can watch artisans create beautiful glass pieces or even take a glass-blowing class yourself. The studio also features a gallery where you can purchase stunning glass art and jewelry.

- **Freak Alley Gallery**: While not directly on 8th Street, this open-air mural gallery is just a short walk away and is a must-see for art lovers. The vibrant murals and street art make it one of Boise's most iconic and Instagram-worthy spots.

DINING ON 8TH STREET

1. Diverse Culinary Options

8th Street is a food lover's paradise, with a wide range of dining options that cater to every taste and budget. From upscale restaurants to casual cafes, the street offers a diverse culinary scene that reflects Boise's growing reputation as a foodie destination.

- **Fork**: A beloved Boise institution, Fork serves American cuisine with a focus on locally sourced ingredients. The menu features everything from hearty burgers to fresh salads, and the outdoor patio is a great spot for people-watching on 8th Street.

- **Bittercreek Alehouse**: This popular pub is known for its extensive selection of craft beers and its commitment to sustainable, farm-to-table fare. The menu includes pub classics like burgers and fish and chips, as well as more adventurous options like bison meatloaf.

- **The Matador**: For those craving Mexican cuisine, The Matador offers a vibrant dining experience with a menu full of flavorful dishes and an impressive selection of tequilas. The street-side patio is perfect for enjoying tacos and margaritas while soaking in the downtown atmosphere.

- **Wild Root Café & Market**: A favorite for health-conscious diners, Wild Root offers a menu focused on fresh, organic ingredients with plenty of vegetarian, vegan, and gluten-free options. The café's bright, modern interior and creative dishes make it a popular brunch spot on 8th Street.

- **Diablo & Sons Saloon**: Offering a modern twist on traditional Western saloons, Diablo & Sons serves up bold flavors with its creative takes on tacos, ribs, and other Southwestern-inspired dishes. The lively atmosphere and unique cocktails make it a great spot for a casual night out.

2. Coffee Shops and Dessert Spots

Whether you're looking for a morning pick-me-up or a sweet treat, 8th Street has you covered with its array of coffee shops and dessert spots.

- **Form & Function**: A specialty coffee shop known for its meticulously brewed coffee and minimalist, modern design. Form & Function is a great place to relax with a cup of coffee, catch up on work, or chat with friends.

- **The STIL (Sweetest Things in Life)**: An artisanal ice cream shop offering a rotating selection of creative flavors, including vegan and alcohol-infused options. The STIL also allows you to pair your ice cream with local beer or wine, making it a unique dessert destination.

- **Java Coffee & Café**: A local favorite, Java offers a cozy atmosphere and a menu full of coffee drinks, smoothies, and light bites. Their "Bowl of Soul" (a rich, spiced chai with espresso) is a must-try for coffee lovers.

ENTERTAINMENT ON 8TH STREET

1. Live Music and Nightlife

8th Street is the epicenter of Boise's nightlife, with a variety of venues offering live music, craft cocktails, and entertainment.

- **Neurolux**: One of Boise's most iconic music venues, Neurolux is a staple of the local music scene. The venue hosts a wide range of live performances, from indie rock bands to electronic DJs, making it a go-to spot for music lovers.

- **The Reef**: A tropical-themed bar and restaurant that features live music several nights a week. The Reef's laid-back vibe and extensive cocktail menu make it a popular spot for both locals and visitors.

- **The Balcony Club**: Located above The Reef, The Balcony Club is Boise's premier LGBTQ+ nightclub, offering a fun and inclusive atmosphere with drag shows, dance parties, and themed events. The outdoor balcony offers great views of downtown Boise.

- **The Basque Center**: Just off 8th Street, The Basque Center is a cultural hub for Boise's Basque community and often hosts traditional Basque dances, live music, and cultural events. It's a unique venue that offers a glimpse into one of Boise's most vibrant cultural traditions.

2. The Egyptian Theatre

While technically located on Main Street, just a block from 8th Street, the **Egyptian Theatre** is a historic gem that's worth a visit. This beautifully restored theater, originally opened in 1927, hosts a variety of events, including film screenings, live performances, and lectures. The Egyptian Theatre's stunning Art Deco architecture and rich history make it a cultural landmark in downtown Boise.

3. Capital City Public Market

On Saturdays from April through December, 8th Street transforms into the bustling **Capital City Public Market**, a lively farmers market that stretches from Bannock Street to the Grove Plaza. The market features a wide array of vendors selling fresh produce, local crafts, artisanal foods, and more. It's a vibrant community event that draws both locals and visitors and offers a great opportunity to sample Boise's local flavors and meet local artisans.

OUTDOOR SPACES AND EVENTS

1. The Grove Plaza

At the southern end of 8th Street, you'll find **The Grove Plaza**, a central gathering place in downtown Boise. The plaza hosts a variety of events throughout the year, including concerts, festivals, and holiday celebrations. It's also a popular spot to relax, enjoy public art installations, and watch the world go by.

2. First Thursday

On the first Thursday of every month, 8th Street and the surrounding downtown area come alive with **First Thursday**, a monthly event that showcases local art, music, and culture. Shops, galleries, and restaurants stay open late, offering special deals, live performances, and art exhibits. It's a great way to experience the creative energy of downtown Boise and discover new local talent.

CHAPTER 4: OUTDOOR ADVENTURES IN BOISE

4.1 BOGUS BASIN: SKIING, SNOWBOARDING, AND HIKING

Nestled in the scenic Boise National Forest, just 16 miles north of downtown Boise, Bogus Basin is a year-round outdoor recreation area that offers some of the best skiing, snowboarding, and hiking in Idaho. With its close proximity to the city, Bogus Basin is a beloved destination for both locals and visitors seeking adventure, natural beauty, and a quick escape into the mountains. Here's everything you need to know about enjoying the outdoor activities at Bogus Basin.

SKIING AND SNOWBOARDING AT BOGUS BASIN

1. Overview

Bogus Basin is one of Idaho's premier ski resorts, offering over 2,600 acres of skiable terrain, making it the second-largest ski area in the state. With its varied terrain, the resort caters to skiers and snowboarders of all levels, from beginners to seasoned experts. The resort's laid-back atmosphere, affordable lift tickets, and stunning mountain views make it a favorite winter destination for those living in or visiting Boise.

2. Terrain and Trails

Bogus Basin's expansive terrain includes 91 named runs, spread across two mountain peaks: Deer Point and Shafer Butte. The resort features a diverse mix of trails, including wide-open groomers, steep chutes, glades, and terrain parks.

- **Beginner Terrain:** The lower mountain offers gentle slopes and dedicated learning areas, perfect for those new to skiing or snowboarding. The "Coach" lift serves an easy green run ideal for first-timers.

- **Intermediate Terrain:** Intermediate skiers and snowboarders will enjoy the abundance of blue runs, with rolling groomers and more challenging trails on both peaks. The "Superior" and "Pine Creek" lifts provide access to some of the most popular intermediate runs.

- **Advanced Terrain:** For advanced and expert riders, Bogus Basin offers thrilling black diamond runs, glades, and even some double-black diamond terrain. The "Superior" lift on the upper mountain is known for its steeper, more challenging runs, including the famous "Paradise" and "The Face."

3. Night Skiing

One of the unique features of Bogus Basin is its extensive night skiing, which allows visitors to hit the slopes after the sun goes down. With over 165 acres of illuminated terrain, Bogus Basin has one of the largest night skiing operations in the Pacific Northwest. This offers a different and exhilarating experience, where you can enjoy the crisp night air and the quiet serenity of the mountains under the lights.

4. Terrain Parks

For those who enjoy freestyle skiing or snowboarding, Bogus Basin has several terrain parks that cater to different skill levels. These parks feature a variety of jumps, rails, boxes, and other features that allow riders to practice their tricks and get creative on the snow. The parks are regularly maintained and updated throughout the season, providing fresh challenges for visitors.

5. Ski and Snowboard Lessons

Bogus Basin is an excellent place to learn how to ski or snowboard, with a dedicated ski school offering lessons for all ages and abilities. Whether you're a first-timer or looking to improve your skills, the resort's experienced instructors provide group and private lessons tailored to your needs. Kids' programs are also available, making it a great destination for family winter fun.

6. Rentals and Services

If you don't have your own gear, Bogus Basin has a well-equipped rental shop that offers skis, snowboards, boots, helmets, and other essential equipment. The rental process is streamlined and easy, allowing you to spend more time on the slopes. Additionally, the resort offers a full-service repair shop for tuning, waxing, and other maintenance needs.

7. Dining and Après-Ski

After a day on the slopes, Bogus Basin offers several dining options where you can warm up and refuel. Simplot Lodge, located at the base area, serves a variety of comfort foods, snacks, and beverages, while Pioneer Lodge on the upper mountain provides a cozy spot with great views and hearty meals. For those who enjoy après-ski, Bogus Basin's Pioneer Lodge Bar offers a selection of beers, wines, and cocktails, making it a perfect place to relax and unwind.

HIKING AT BOGUS BASIN

1. Summer and Fall Hiking

When the snow melts, Bogus Basin transforms into a paradise for hikers, offering miles of trails that wind through the lush forest, wildflower meadows, and rocky ridges of the Boise Mountains. The resort's elevation provides cooler temperatures during the summer months, making it an ideal escape from the heat of the valley below.

- **Shafer Butte Trail**: One of the most popular hikes at Bogus Basin, the Shafer Butte Trail offers stunning views of the surrounding mountains and valleys. The trailhead is located near Pioneer Lodge and offers a moderately challenging hike that takes you to the summit of Shafer Butte, the highest point in the Boise Ridge at over 7,500 feet. The panoramic views from the top are breathtaking, especially at sunrise or sunset.

- **Mores Mountain Loop**: This family-friendly loop trail is a favorite among locals for its relatively easy terrain and beautiful scenery. The 2.5-mile loop takes you through forests of Douglas fir and ponderosa pine, with several scenic overlooks along the way. The trail is also known for its vibrant wildflowers in late spring and early summer.

- **Stack Rock Trail**: Located a bit further from the main Bogus Basin area, the Stack Rock Trail is a moderately difficult hike that leads to a unique rock formation resembling a giant stack of pancakes. The trail is about 9 miles round trip and offers stunning views of the Boise foothills and beyond. It's a great choice for those looking for a longer hike with a rewarding destination.

2. Mountain Biking

Bogus Basin is also a popular destination for mountain biking, with a network of trails that cater to riders of all skill levels. The resort offers both cross-country and downhill trails, with varying levels of difficulty. During the summer, the Deer Point Express lift is equipped to carry bikes, allowing riders to access the downhill trails without the climb.

- **Around the Mountain Trail**: A favorite among mountain bikers, this 10-mile loop offers a mix of smooth singletrack, rocky sections, and stunning views. The trail circumnavigates the upper slopes of Bogus Basin, providing a challenging yet rewarding ride.

- **Downhill Trails**: For those seeking an adrenaline rush, Bogus Basin's downhill trails offer fast descents, berms, jumps, and technical features. The resort's bike park is designed to challenge even the most experienced riders, while still offering trails suitable for intermediate riders.

3. Guided Hikes and Educational Programs

Bogus Basin offers guided hikes and educational programs during the summer and fall, providing visitors with the opportunity to learn about the local flora, fauna, and geology. These guided hikes are led by knowledgeable naturalists who share insights into the unique ecosystems of the Boise Mountains, making them a great way to enhance your outdoor experience.

4. Scenic Chairlift Rides

For those who want to enjoy the views without the hike, Bogus Basin offers scenic chairlift rides during the summer months. The Deer Point Express lift takes you to the top of Deer Point, where you can take in panoramic views of the Treasure Valley, the Boise National Forest, and the distant Owyhee Mountains. It's a relaxing way to experience the beauty of Bogus Basin, especially if you're short on time or prefer a more leisurely adventure.

YEAR-ROUND EVENTS AND ACTIVITIES

Bogus Basin hosts a variety of events throughout the year, from mountain festivals and live music to races and competitions. These events add to the vibrant community atmosphere of the resort and offer something for everyone, whether you're a participant or a spectator.

- **Bogus Basin Mountain Festival**: Held annually in the summer, this festival features live music, food vendors, outdoor activities, and family-friendly fun. It's a great way to experience the lively community spirit of Bogus Basin while enjoying the beautiful mountain scenery.

- **Winter Events**: During the winter season, Bogus Basin hosts ski and snowboard races, freestyle competitions, and fun community events like torchlight parades and holiday celebrations. These events bring together skiers and snowboarders of all ages and abilities, creating a festive atmosphere on the mountain.

4.2 BOISE FOOTHILLS: TRAILS FOR ALL LEVELS

The Boise Foothills are a cherished natural playground, offering an extensive network of trails that cater to hikers, bikers, and outdoor enthusiasts of all skill levels. Just minutes from downtown Boise, these rolling hills provide a serene escape with stunning views, diverse landscapes, and a variety of trail experiences. Whether you're a seasoned hiker looking for a challenging trek or a beginner seeking a peaceful walk in nature, the Boise Foothills have something for everyone. Here's a guide to some of the best trails for all levels.

BEGINNER TRAILS

1. Hulls Gulch Interpretive Trail

- **Distance**: 3.7 miles (round trip)

- **Elevation Gain**: 500 feet

- **Trailhead**: Hulls Gulch Trailhead

The Hulls Gulch Interpretive Trail is one of the most popular beginner-friendly trails in the Boise Foothills. This well-maintained, out-and-back trail offers a gentle ascent through scenic landscapes, including sagebrush-covered hills, riparian areas, and shaded creek crossings. Along the way, interpretive signs provide insights into the local flora, fauna, and geology, making it an educational as well as an enjoyable hike.

The trail is perfect for families and beginners, with its moderate distance and gentle elevation gain. It's also dog-friendly, so feel free to bring along your furry friend (on a leash). The trail culminates at the junction with the Upper Hulls Gulch Trail, where you can enjoy views of the surrounding foothills and downtown Boise in the distance.

2. Camel's Back Park to Lower Hulls Gulch Trail

- **Distance**: 2.5 miles (round trip)

- **Elevation Gain**: 400 feet

- **Trailhead**: Camel's Back Park

Camel's Back Park is a popular starting point for many trails in the Boise Foothills, and the Lower Hulls Gulch Trail is an excellent option for beginners. Starting from the park's parking lot, this easy-to-follow trail winds its way through the lower foothills, offering a mix of open meadows and shaded creekside sections.

The trail is well-suited for a leisurely walk or a short hike, with minimal elevation gain and a well-maintained path. It's also a favorite among trail runners and mountain bikers. The views of downtown Boise and the surrounding foothills make this trail a great introduction to the area's natural beauty.

3. Owl's Roost Trail

- **Distance**: 1.6 miles (round trip)

- **Elevation Gain**: 150 feet

- **Trailhead**: Hulls Gulch Trailhead

The Owl's Roost Trail is another excellent beginner-friendly option in the Boise Foothills. This short, loop trail offers a peaceful walk through rolling hills and juniper groves. The trail is relatively flat and wide, making it suitable for hikers of all ages and abilities.

The Owl's Roost Trail connects with several other trails in the area, including Kestrel Trail and Red Fox Trail, allowing you to extend your hike if you wish. The gentle terrain and beautiful scenery make this trail a favorite for those looking for a quick escape into nature.

INTERMEDIATE TRAILS

1. Table Rock Trail

- **Distance**: 3.7 miles (round trip)

- **Elevation Gain**: 900 feet

- **Trailhead**: Old Penitentiary Trailhead

The Table Rock Trail is one of Boise's most iconic hikes, offering spectacular views of the city and the surrounding Treasure Valley. The trail begins at the Old Penitentiary Trailhead and ascends steeply to the summit of Table Rock, a prominent sandstone plateau that overlooks Boise.

While the trail is relatively short, the steep elevation gain makes it a challenging hike for beginners but a perfect fit for those with some hiking experience. The reward at the top is well worth the effort, with panoramic views that stretch across the valley to the Owyhee Mountains in the distance.

The trail is popular, especially during sunrise and sunset, so expect to share the path with other hikers. There are several routes to the top, so you can choose a more direct path or a longer, more gradual ascent depending on your preference.

2. Military Reserve Loop

- **Distance**: 5.4 miles (loop)

- **Elevation Gain**: 650 feet

- **Trailhead**: Military Reserve Park

The Military Reserve Loop is an excellent intermediate trail that offers a variety of terrain and great views of the Boise Foothills. This loop trail starts at the Military Reserve Trailhead and takes you through rolling hills, open meadows, and along the Cottonwood Creek.

The loop includes several connecting trails, such as the Cottonwood Creek Trail, Eagle Ridge Trail, and Central Ridge Trail, allowing you to customize your hike based on your desired distance and difficulty. The trail is moderately challenging, with some sections that require a bit of climbing, but it's well-maintained and easy to follow.

This trail is popular with both hikers and mountain bikers, so be prepared to share the trail. The Military Reserve Loop offers a fantastic way to experience the diverse landscapes of the Boise Foothills.

3. Dry Creek Trail

- **Distance**: 7 miles (round trip)

- **Elevation Gain**: 1,000 feet

- **Trailhead**: Dry Creek Trailhead

The Dry Creek Trail is a beautiful and moderately challenging hike that takes you deep into the Boise Foothills. The trail follows Dry Creek through a lush, forested canyon, offering a cool and shaded hike even on warmer days. The trail is popular for its scenic beauty, with the sound of the creek accompanying you for much of the hike.

The trail is relatively narrow and can be rocky in places, making it more suitable for intermediate hikers. The elevation gain is gradual, and the trail offers a mix of open meadows and forested sections, with several creek crossings along the way.

The Dry Creek Trail can be extended into a longer hike by connecting with the Shingle Creek Trail or the Dry Creek-Shingle Creek Loop, providing more options for those seeking a full-day adventure.

ADVANCED TRAILS

1. Ridge to Rivers Trail

- **Distance**: 12 miles (point-to-point)

- **Elevation Gain**: 1,500 feet

- **Trailhead**: Various access points, including Camel's Back Park and 8th Street Extension

The Ridge to Rivers Trail is part of Boise's extensive Ridge to Rivers trail system, which spans over 200 miles of interconnected trails. This specific route is a challenging, point-to-point trail that traverses the ridge of the Boise Foothills, offering stunning panoramic views of the Treasure Valley and the Boise River below.

This trail is ideal for experienced hikers looking for a longer and more challenging trek. The trail includes steep climbs, rocky sections, and some exposed ridges, making it a true test of endurance. Along the way, you'll be rewarded with sweeping vistas, wildflower-covered hillsides in the spring, and the solitude of the high desert.

You can start the trail from various access points, including Camel's Back Park or the 8th Street Extension. Because it's a point-to-point trail, you'll need to arrange transportation back to your starting point, or you can turn around at a designated point to make it a round-trip hike.

2. Stack Rock Trail

- **Distance**: 9 miles (round trip)

- **Elevation Gain**: 1,500 feet

- **Trailhead**: Freddy's Stack Rock Trailhead (Bogus Basin Road)

The Stack Rock Trail is a favorite among experienced hikers and offers a challenging yet rewarding hike to one of the most unique natural features in the Boise Foothills—Stack Rock, a towering granite formation that resembles a stack of pancakes.

The trail begins off Bogus Basin Road and takes you through dense forests, open meadows, and rocky outcrops. The trail is well-marked but involves a steady climb, making it more suitable for advanced hikers. The final stretch to Stack Rock requires some scrambling over rocks, but the view from the top is well worth the effort.

From the summit, you can enjoy panoramic views of the surrounding foothills, the Treasure Valley, and the distant mountains. The trail is a fantastic option for those looking to combine a good workout with breathtaking scenery.

3. Five Mile Gulch to Watchman Trail Loop

- **Distance**: 10.5 miles (loop)

- **Elevation Gain**: 2,200 feet

- **Trailhead**: Five Mile Gulch Trailhead

The Five Mile Gulch to Watchman Trail Loop is a challenging hike that offers some of the best views in the Boise Foothills. The loop takes you through a variety of landscapes, including steep gulches, ridgelines, and expansive valleys.

The trail begins with a steep ascent up Five Mile Gulch, leading to a ridge with sweeping views of the foothills and beyond. From there, the trail continues along the Watchman Trail, which offers a mix of challenging climbs and descents. The trail is well-marked but requires good fitness and endurance due to its length and elevation gain.

The loop is a favorite among advanced hikers and trail runners looking for a challenging workout with plenty of rewards in terms of scenery. The Watchman Trail is particularly stunning in the spring, when wildflowers blanket the hillsides.

4.3 RAFTING AND KAYAKING ON THE BOISE RIVER

The Boise River is a central part of the outdoor lifestyle in Idaho's capital city, offering a perfect setting for rafting and kayaking. Flowing through the heart of Boise, the river provides both tranquil and thrilling experiences, making it a popular destination for locals and visitors alike. Whether you're seeking a leisurely float or an adrenaline-pumping ride, the Boise River has something to offer for everyone. Here's a guide to rafting and kayaking on the Boise River, including where to go, what to expect, and how to make the most of your river adventure.

THE BOISE RIVER: A QUICK OVERVIEW

The Boise River originates in the Sawtooth Mountains and flows through the Treasure Valley, eventually joining the Snake River. In Boise, the river is a key feature of the city's landscape, with the Boise River Greenbelt running alongside it, providing easy access to the water for recreational activities.

The river's flow is regulated by a series of dams, which means water levels can vary depending on the time of year. Typically, spring and early summer see higher flows due to snowmelt, making it an ideal time for more challenging kayaking and rafting. By late summer, the river's flow slows down, creating perfect conditions for a relaxed float.

RAFTING ON THE BOISE RIVER

1. Family-Friendly Floating

One of the most popular activities on the Boise River is family-friendly floating. The river's gentle current and scenic surroundings make it an ideal place for a relaxing day on the water. The stretch of river from Barber Park to Ann Morrison Park is the most popular section for floating and is suitable for all ages and skill levels.

- **Starting Point: Barber Park**: Barber Park, located just southeast of downtown Boise, is the primary launch point for river floats. The park offers a convenient shuttle service, tube and raft rentals, and facilities like restrooms and picnic areas.

- **The Float Route**: The float from Barber Park to Ann Morrison Park covers approximately six miles and takes about 2-3 hours, depending on the flow of the river. Along the way, you'll enjoy views of lush greenery, sandy beaches, and wildlife such as birds and fish. The float includes a few small rapids, which add a bit of excitement without being too challenging.

- **Safety Tips**: While the float is generally safe and suitable for beginners, it's important to wear a life jacket at all times and be aware of your surroundings. The river is popular during the summer months, so expect to share the water with other floaters, kayakers, and paddleboarders.

2. Rafting Trips for Thrill-Seekers

For those seeking a bit more excitement, the Boise River also offers sections with faster currents and small rapids that are perfect for a more adventurous rafting experience. While the main section through Boise is relatively calm, you can find more challenging conditions upstream or on nearby rivers like the Payette River.

- **Whitewater Rafting on the Payette River**: Just a short drive from Boise, the Payette River offers some of the best whitewater rafting in the region. With rapids ranging from Class II to Class IV, the Payette provides a thrilling experience for both novice and experienced rafters. Several local outfitters offer guided rafting trips on the Payette, making it a great option for those looking to combine their Boise River float with a more intense whitewater adventure.

KAYAKING ON THE BOISE RIVER

1. Recreational Kayaking

Kayaking on the Boise River is a fantastic way to explore the water at your own pace. The river's gentle flow and scenic beauty make it an ideal spot for recreational kayaking, whether you're a beginner or an experienced paddler.

- **Best Sections for Kayaking**: The stretch from Barber Park to Ann Morrison Park is also popular with kayakers. This section offers a mix of calm water and mild rapids, making it perfect for a leisurely paddle. The numerous access points along the Boise River Greenbelt allow you to tailor your trip to your desired distance and time on the water.

- **Wildlife and Scenery**: As you paddle along the river, keep an eye out for the local wildlife, including deer, beavers, and a variety of birds such as herons and osprey. The riverbanks are lined with trees and vegetation, providing a peaceful and picturesque backdrop for your kayaking adventure.

2. Whitewater Kayaking at Boise River Whitewater Park

For those who are more experienced or seeking a challenge, the **Boise River Whitewater Park** offers a thrilling urban kayaking experience. Located near downtown Boise, this engineered section of the river features adjustable waves and rapids that are perfect for whitewater kayaking and surfing.

- **Features of the Whitewater Park**: The park's waves can be adjusted to create different levels of difficulty, from beginner-friendly waves to more advanced whitewater features. The park is popular with kayakers and surfers, and it's a great place to practice your skills or simply watch others take on the waves.

- **Access and Facilities**: The Whitewater Park is easily accessible from the Greenbelt and features parking, restrooms, and nearby dining options. The park is also a hub for community events and competitions, adding to its lively and energetic atmosphere.

3. Guided Kayaking Tours

If you're new to kayaking or prefer a guided experience, several local outfitters offer guided kayaking tours on the Boise River. These tours provide all the necessary equipment, safety instructions, and knowledgeable guides who can share insights about the river's history, ecology, and wildlife.

- **Types of Tours**: Guided tours range from short, leisurely paddles suitable for families to longer, more adventurous trips that explore less-traveled sections of the river. Some tours also include opportunities for birdwatching, photography, or even a riverside picnic.

PLANNING YOUR BOISE RIVER ADVENTURE

1. Rentals and Gear

If you don't have your own gear, there are several rental shops in Boise that offer everything you need for a day on the river, including rafts, kayaks, tubes, life jackets, and paddles. Many of these rental shops are located near Barber Park, making it easy to pick up your gear and get on the water.

2. Shuttle Services

To make your river adventure as convenient as possible, shuttle services are available to transport you and your gear from the take-out point at Ann Morrison Park back to Barber Park. This allows you to enjoy the river without worrying about the logistics of getting back to your starting point.

3. Safety Considerations

While the Boise River is generally safe for recreational activities, it's important to take some basic safety precautions:

- **Wear a Life Jacket**: Always wear a life jacket, regardless of your swimming ability. The current can be stronger than it appears, and a life jacket is your best protection in case of an accident.

- **Check Water Conditions**: Before heading out, check the river's flow and conditions. High water levels in the spring can create stronger currents and more challenging conditions, while low water levels in late summer can expose rocks and other hazards.

- **Respect the River**: Be mindful of other river users, including anglers, swimmers, and other paddlers. Keep your distance from wildlife, and avoid disturbing the natural environment.

4. Best Time to Go

The best time for rafting and kayaking on the Boise River is from late spring to early fall, when the weather is warm and the water levels are ideal for recreation. The river is most popular during the summer months, especially on weekends, so plan to arrive early if you want to avoid the crowds.

4.4 Day Trips: Discover Idaho's Natural Beauty

Idaho is a state blessed with diverse landscapes, from rugged mountains and serene lakes to vast deserts and lush forests. Just a short drive from Boise, you can explore some of the most stunning natural beauty that Idaho has to offer. Whether you're looking for a peaceful retreat or an adventurous outing, these day trips will allow you to discover the incredible outdoor treasures that make Idaho a paradise for nature lovers.

1. Sawtooth National Recreation Area

Distance from Boise: Approximately 2.5 hours (130 miles)

The Sawtooth National Recreation Area (SNRA) is a breathtaking destination that showcases some of Idaho's most iconic mountain scenery. Located in central Idaho, the SNRA covers over 756,000 acres and includes more than 700 miles of trails, 300 alpine lakes, and the rugged peaks of the Sawtooth Mountains.

- **Hiking and Backpacking**: The SNRA offers a wide range of hiking trails, from easy walks to challenging multi-day backpacking trips. Popular hikes include the trail to Alice Lake, which offers stunning views of jagged peaks and pristine waters, and the Iron Creek to Sawtooth Lake trail, where you can explore one of the most photographed lakes in Idaho.

- **Scenic Drives**: If you prefer to take in the scenery from your car, the Sawtooth Scenic Byway is a must. This drive takes you through the heart of the SNRA, offering panoramic views of the mountains, rivers, and meadows. Stop at Stanley Lake for a picnic or take a detour to Redfish Lake for a swim.

- **Wildlife Watching**: The SNRA is home to a variety of wildlife, including elk, deer, black bears, and bald eagles. Keep your camera ready as you explore the area, especially in the early morning or late evening when animals are most active.

2. BRUNEAU DUNES STATE PARK

Distance from Boise: Approximately 1.5 hours (65 miles)

Bruneau Dunes State Park is home to the tallest single-structured sand dune in North America, towering 470 feet above the surrounding desert. This unique landscape offers a stark contrast to the mountainous regions of Idaho and provides an exciting day trip for those looking to explore something different.

- **Dune Climbing**: Climbing the towering dunes is a challenging but rewarding experience. The views from the top are spectacular, with the vast expanse of the desert stretching out before you. Be sure to bring plenty of water and prepare for the heat, especially in the summer.

- **Sandboarding**: For a fun and adventurous activity, try sandboarding down the dunes. You can rent sandboards at the park's visitor center and enjoy sliding down the steep slopes of soft sand.

- **Stargazing**: Bruneau Dunes State Park is also known for its incredible night skies. The park's observatory offers public stargazing programs on weekends during the summer months, allowing you to explore the stars and planets with the help of powerful telescopes.

3. SHOSHONE FALLS

Distance from Boise: Approximately 2 hours (130 miles)

Often referred to as the "Niagara of the West," Shoshone Falls is one of the most impressive natural wonders in Idaho. Located on the Snake River near

Twin Falls, Shoshone Falls is actually higher than Niagara Falls, plunging 212 feet over a 900-foot-wide span.

- **Waterfall Viewing**: The best time to visit Shoshone Falls is in the spring when water flow is at its peak, creating a thunderous display of cascading water. The park offers several viewing platforms where you can take in the stunning sight of the falls and the surrounding canyon.

- **Picnicking and Hiking**: The park surrounding Shoshone Falls is a great place to spend a day with family or friends. Enjoy a picnic with views of the falls, or take a short hike along the trails that offer different perspectives of the falls and the Snake River.

- **Kayaking and Paddleboarding**: For a unique view of the falls, consider kayaking or paddleboarding on the Snake River below the falls. There are rental options available in the nearby town of Twin Falls, allowing you to explore the river and get up close to this natural wonder.

4. HELLS CANYON NATIONAL RECREATION AREA

Distance from Boise: Approximately 3 hours (140 miles)

Hells Canyon is North America's deepest river gorge, plunging to depths of nearly 8,000 feet. This awe-inspiring canyon, carved by the Snake River, offers rugged beauty and a sense of remote wilderness that makes it a perfect destination for adventurous day-trippers.

- **Jet Boat Tours**: One of the best ways to experience Hells Canyon is by taking a jet boat tour on the Snake River. These tours take you deep into the canyon, where you'll encounter dramatic cliffs, ancient petroglyphs, and an abundance of wildlife. The tours offer a thrilling ride and breathtaking scenery.

- **Hiking and Wildlife Watching**: The Hells Canyon area offers numerous hiking trails that range from easy to challenging. The Seven Devils Loop, accessible from the Idaho side, offers spectacular views of the canyon and the surrounding mountains. Keep an eye out for wildlife, including bighorn sheep, eagles, and black bears.

- **Fishing**: Hells Canyon is also a popular spot for fishing, particularly for smallmouth bass and sturgeon. The Snake River's deep waters and remote location provide excellent fishing opportunities, whether you're casting from the shore or from a boat.

5. CITY OF ROCKS NATIONAL RESERVE

Distance from Boise: Approximately 3 hours (180 miles)

City of Rocks National Reserve is a paradise for rock climbers, hikers, and history buffs alike. This unique landscape, located in southern Idaho near the Utah border, is characterized by massive granite formations that rise dramatically from the high desert.

- **Rock Climbing**: City of Rocks is renowned for its world-class rock climbing, with routes ranging from beginner-friendly climbs to challenging technical routes. The area attracts climbers from around the world, and the stunning rock formations provide a spectacular backdrop for your ascent.

- **Hiking and Exploring**: For those who prefer to keep their feet on the ground, City of Rocks offers several hiking trails that take you through the reserve's striking landscape. The Bath Rock Trail is a short, easy hike that offers excellent views of the rock formations and surrounding desert.

- **Historic Sites**: The reserve is also rich in history, with evidence of Native American habitation and pioneer trails. The California Trail, used by thousands of pioneers during the westward expansion, passes through the area. You can see wagon ruts and inscriptions left by travelers on the rocks, offering a glimpse into the past.

6. LAKE CASCADE STATE PARK

Distance from Boise: Approximately 2 hours (75 miles)

Lake Cascade, located in the mountains of central Idaho, is a beautiful destination for water-based recreation and outdoor relaxation. The lake's serene waters and surrounding forests make it a perfect spot for a day trip filled with fun and tranquility.

- **Boating and Fishing**: Lake Cascade is a popular spot for boating, with several boat ramps and marinas providing easy access to the water. The lake is also known for its excellent fishing, with species like rainbow trout, smallmouth bass, and perch available for anglers.

- **Swimming and Picnicking**: The park's numerous beaches and picnic areas make it a great place to spend a day with family. Enjoy a swim in the cool, clear waters of the lake, or relax on the beach with a picnic and take in the stunning mountain views.

- **Hiking and Wildlife Viewing**: Lake Cascade State Park offers several hiking trails that take you through the surrounding forests and along the lakeshore. The area is home to a variety of wildlife, including deer, elk, and bald eagles, making it a great destination for nature lovers.

7. THE OWYHEE CANYONLANDS

Distance from Boise: Approximately 2.5 hours (110 miles)

The Owyhee Canyonlands, located in the remote southwestern corner of Idaho, is one of the state's most rugged and spectacular landscapes. This vast, wild area is characterized by deep canyons, towering rock spires, and wide-open spaces, offering a true sense of solitude and adventure.

- **Hiking and Exploration**: The Owyhee Canyonlands offer endless opportunities for hiking and exploration. Trails like the Painted Canyon Loop and the Leslie Gulch Trail take you through some of the most dramatic scenery in the area, with colorful rock formations, narrow slot canyons, and expansive desert vistas.

- **Photography**: The Owyhee Canyonlands are a photographer's dream, with their otherworldly landscapes and dramatic light. Early morning and late afternoon are the best times to capture the area's stunning colors and shadows.

- **Camping and Stargazing**: For those looking to extend their day trip into an overnight adventure, the Owyhee Canyonlands offer several primitive camping spots where you can enjoy the area's incredible night skies. The lack of light pollution makes this one of the best stargazing destinations in Idaho.

CHAPTER 5: FAMILY-FRIENDLY ACTIVITIES

5.1 ZOO BOISE: WILDLIFE ENCOUNTERS

Zoo Boise is a beloved destination for families in Idaho's capital city, offering a fun and educational experience where visitors of all ages can connect with wildlife from around the world. Located in the heart of Julia Davis Park, Zoo Boise provides a variety of interactive exhibits, animal encounters, and special events that make it a must-visit attraction for both locals and tourists. Here's a guide to the best of what Zoo Boise has to offer for a memorable family day out.

1. OVERVIEW OF ZOO BOISE

Zoo Boise is home to over 300 animals representing more than 100 species from around the globe. The zoo is dedicated to education, conservation, and the preservation of wildlife, making it a place where visitors can learn about the importance of protecting the natural world while enjoying close encounters with fascinating creatures.

The zoo is designed with families in mind, featuring easy-to-navigate pathways, interactive exhibits, and plenty of shaded areas for rest and relaxation. With its mix of exotic animals, local wildlife, and hands-on experiences, Zoo Boise offers something for everyone, from toddlers to grandparents.

2. MUST-SEE EXHIBITS

a. African Plains

The African Plains exhibit is one of Zoo Boise's most popular attractions, offering visitors a glimpse into the wildlife of Africa's savannas. Here, you can observe majestic animals like giraffes, zebras, and African lions in environments that mimic their natural habitats.

- **Giraffe Encounter**: One of the highlights of the African Plains is the opportunity to get up close and personal with giraffes. The Giraffe Encounter allows visitors to feed these gentle giants, offering a unique and unforgettable experience for children and adults alike.

- **Lions and Warthogs**: Watch as African lions lounge in the sun or playfully interact with each other, while nearby, warthogs dig and explore their habitat. The exhibit provides excellent viewing opportunities and educational information about these iconic African species.

b. Butterflies in Bloom

During the warmer months, Zoo Boise's **Butterflies in Bloom** exhibit is a must-visit. This seasonal exhibit immerses visitors in a vibrant garden filled with colorful butterflies from around the world. Walk through the lush, flower-filled enclosure as butterflies flutter around, landing on plants and sometimes even on visitors.

- **Educational Experience**: The exhibit is not only beautiful but also educational, with staff on hand to provide information about the life cycle of butterflies, their role in ecosystems, and the importance of conservation efforts to protect these delicate creatures.

c. Primate World

Primate World is a favorite among visitors, showcasing a variety of primates, including monkeys, lemurs, and gibbons. The exhibit is designed to mimic the natural habitats of these intelligent and social animals, offering plenty of opportunities to observe their behaviors up close.

- **Lemur Island**: One of the standout features of Primate World is Lemur Island, where visitors can watch playful lemurs leap and climb in their spacious outdoor enclosure. The island's design allows the lemurs to display their natural behaviors, making it a fun and educational experience for all ages.

- **Gibbons and Spider Monkeys**: Watch as gibbons swing gracefully from branch to branch and spider monkeys use their prehensile tails to navigate their environment. These primates are always active, providing endless entertainment for zoo-goers.

d. Conservation Cruise

The Conservation Cruise is a unique feature of Zoo Boise that combines fun with education. Hop on a boat and take a leisurely cruise around the zoo's lagoon, where you'll learn about conservation efforts both locally and globally. The cruise is a relaxing way to see parts of the zoo from a different perspective while gaining insight into the important work being done to protect wildlife.

e. Small Animal Kingdom

The Small Animal Kingdom is home to a variety of smaller species from around the world, including reptiles, amphibians, birds, and mammals. This indoor exhibit allows visitors to get up close to animals like meerkats, red pandas, and exotic birds.

- **Meerkat Manor**: The meerkats are always a hit with families, as these curious creatures are constantly digging, exploring, and standing on their hind legs to survey their surroundings. The exhibit is designed to allow children to get a close look at the meerkats through viewing tunnels and windows.

- **Reptile House**: The Reptile House within the Small Animal Kingdom showcases a variety of snakes, lizards, and turtles. It's a great place for children to learn about these fascinating creatures and overcome any fears they might have about reptiles.

3. INTERACTIVE EXPERIENCES AND ANIMAL ENCOUNTERS

Zoo Boise offers a range of interactive experiences that allow visitors to engage with the animals in unique and memorable ways. These experiences are designed to enhance your visit and provide deeper connections with the zoo's residents.

a. Sloth Bear Encounter

For a truly unforgettable experience, book a **Sloth Bear Encounter**, where you can meet the zoo's resident sloth bears up close. During this encounter, you'll learn about the care and feeding of sloth bears, and you may even have the chance to help prepare their food or participate in enrichment activities that keep the bears mentally stimulated.

b. Animal Presentations

Throughout the day, Zoo Boise offers animal presentations where zookeepers introduce visitors to different animals and share interesting facts about their behaviors, diets, and conservation status. These presentations are interactive and often allow for questions and close-up views of the animals.

c. Zoo Farm

The Zoo Farm is a hands-on area where children can interact with domesticated farm animals like goats, sheep, and chickens. Kids can pet and feed the animals, making it a favorite spot for young visitors. The Zoo Farm also features educational displays about farming, animal care, and the importance of agriculture.

4. CONSERVATION AND EDUCATION

Zoo Boise is not just about entertainment; it's also deeply committed to conservation and education. The zoo participates in several global conservation initiatives, focusing on protecting endangered species and their habitats. A portion of every admission ticket goes directly to support conservation projects, meaning your visit helps make a difference.

- **Zoo Boise Conservation Fund**: The Conservation Fund supports various projects worldwide, including efforts to protect elephants in Africa, snow leopards in Asia, and frogs in Central America. The zoo also partners with local organizations to conserve Idaho's native wildlife.

- **Educational Programs**: Zoo Boise offers a variety of educational programs for children and adults, including summer camps, school field trips, and family workshops. These programs are designed to foster a love of nature and wildlife conservation in participants of all ages.

5. SPECIAL EVENTS AND SEASONAL ACTIVITIES

Zoo Boise hosts a variety of special events throughout the year, many of which are geared towards families and children. These events add an extra layer of fun to your visit and often include themed activities, special animal encounters, and seasonal decorations.

- **Boo at the Zoo**: Held every October, Boo at the Zoo is a family-friendly Halloween event where children can trick-or-treat around the zoo, enjoy Halloween-themed animal presentations, and participate in costume contests. The zoo is decorated for the occasion, making it a spooky yet fun experience.

- **Easter EGGstravaganza**: Celebrate Easter at Zoo Boise with an egg hunt, spring-themed crafts, and opportunities to meet the Easter Bunny. This event is a hit with families and provides a festive way to welcome the spring season.

- **Zoo Daze**: Zoo Daze is a summer celebration featuring special activities, games, and animal encounters. It's a great time to visit the zoo, as the animals are often more active in the warmer months.

6. DINING AND AMENITIES

Zoo Boise offers several dining options where you can grab a bite to eat during your visit. The zoo's main café serves a variety of snacks, sandwiches, and beverages, and there are picnic areas where you can enjoy your meal outdoors.

- **Concessions**: In addition to the café, you'll find several concession stands throughout the zoo offering ice cream, popcorn, and other treats. These are perfect for a quick snack break as you explore the exhibits.

- **Gift Shop**: Before you leave, be sure to stop by the zoo's gift shop, where you can purchase souvenirs, toys, and educational materials. A portion of the proceeds from the gift shop also supports Zoo Boise's conservation efforts.

7. PLANNING YOUR VISIT

Zoo Boise is open year-round, with hours varying depending on the season. The zoo is accessible for strollers and wheelchairs, and rental options are available on-site. To make the most of your visit, consider arriving early in the day when the animals are most active and the zoo is less crowded.

- **Admission and Membership**: Admission prices are affordable, and the zoo offers discounts for children, seniors, and military personnel. If you're a frequent visitor, consider purchasing a membership, which provides unlimited access to the zoo for a year and additional perks like discounts on events and in the gift shop.

- **Parking**: Parking is available in Julia Davis Park, with several lots located near the zoo's entrance. Parking is free, but it can fill up quickly on weekends and during special events, so plan to arrive early or consider alternative transportation options, such as biking along the Boise River Greenbelt.

5.2 DISCOVERY CENTER OF IDAHO: HANDS-ON LEARNING

The Discovery Center of Idaho (DCI) is a dynamic science center located in the heart of Boise, offering interactive exhibits and hands-on learning experiences that engage visitors of all ages. With its focus on making science accessible and fun, the Discovery Center of Idaho is a favorite destination for families, school groups, and curious minds eager to explore the wonders of science, technology, engineering, and mathematics (STEM). Here's an overview of what you can expect during your visit to this educational and entertaining facility.

1. OVERVIEW OF THE DISCOVERY CENTER OF IDAHO

Founded in 1988, the Discovery Center of Idaho has been inspiring curiosity and a love for science for over three decades. The center's mission is to stimulate interest in science through interactive exhibits and programs that encourage exploration, experimentation, and discovery. With over 200 hands-on exhibits, DCI provides a place where visitors can learn by doing, making it an ideal environment for both children and adults to engage with scientific concepts in a tangible and memorable way.

2. INTERACTIVE EXHIBITS

The heart of the Discovery Center of Idaho lies in its interactive exhibits, which cover a broad range of scientific topics, from physics and engineering to biology and earth science. These exhibits are designed to be touched, manipulated, and explored, allowing visitors to learn through direct experience.

a. Physics and Motion

- **Bernoulli Blower**: This popular exhibit demonstrates the principles of air pressure and lift. Visitors can experiment with floating balls in a stream of air, discovering how changes in airspeed and pressure affect the ball's movement.

- **Giant Lever**: Explore the concept of mechanical advantage by lifting heavy objects with the help of a giant lever. This hands-on exhibit shows how simple machines can make work easier, providing a concrete understanding of physics in action.

- **Pendulum Painting**: Create your own art using the power of physics! This exhibit allows you to release a pendulum with paint attached to it, creating patterns that demonstrate the forces at play.

b. Engineering and Design

- **Build a Bridge**: In this exhibit, visitors are challenged to design and construct a bridge using various materials. Test your creation's strength and stability, learning about engineering principles such as tension, compression, and load distribution.

- **Kaleidoscope**: Discover the beauty of symmetry and geometric design by creating your own patterns with a giant kaleidoscope. This exhibit encourages creativity while demonstrating the principles of reflection and optics.

- **LEGO Station**: This exhibit invites visitors to build and test their own structures using LEGO bricks. From skyscrapers to bridges, this station is perfect for budding engineers to explore architectural concepts through play.

c. Biology and Life Sciences

- **Human Body Exhibit**: Dive into the fascinating world of human biology with exhibits that explore the systems and functions of the human body. Interactive displays allow visitors to learn about the circulatory, respiratory, and digestive systems, as well as how the brain controls the body's movements and senses.

- **Plant and Animal Life**: Explore the diversity of life on Earth through exhibits that focus on the biology of plants and animals. Learn about ecosystems, food chains, and the adaptations that allow different species to survive and thrive in various environments.

d. Earth Science and Space

- **Seismic Table**: Experience the power of an earthquake at the seismic table, where you can build structures and see how they withstand the forces of simulated seismic activity. This exhibit teaches about tectonic plates, earthquake safety, and the science of building design.

- **Planetary Exploration**: Travel through the solar system with exhibits that explore the planets, moons, and other celestial bodies. Learn about the formation of the solar system, the conditions on different planets, and the ongoing exploration of space.

e. Special Exhibits

In addition to its permanent exhibits, the Discovery Center of Idaho regularly hosts special exhibits that bring new and exciting topics to the center. These traveling exhibits often focus on specific themes, such as robotics, dinosaurs, or the science of sports, and they provide fresh opportunities for learning and exploration. Be sure to check the center's schedule to see what special exhibits are currently on display during your visit.

3. HANDS-ON WORKSHOPS AND PROGRAMS

The Discovery Center of Idaho offers a variety of hands-on workshops and educational programs designed to deepen visitors' understanding of science and technology. These programs are available for all ages and often tie into the center's exhibits, providing a more in-depth exploration of specific topics.

a. STEM Camps

- **Summer Camps**: DCI's summer camps are a hit with kids, offering week-long programs that focus on different STEM topics such as robotics, coding, chemistry, and environmental science. These camps combine fun activities with educational content, encouraging kids to explore and experiment in a supportive environment.

- **Holiday and School Break Camps**: In addition to summer camps, the center also offers camps during school holidays and breaks. These camps provide hands-on learning opportunities while keeping kids engaged and entertained during their time off from school.

b. Workshops and Classes

- **Family Workshops**: These workshops are designed for families to learn and create together. Topics might include building rockets, creating chemical reactions, or exploring the science of sound. Family workshops are a great way to spend quality time together while learning something new.

- **Adult Programs**: The Discovery Center of Idaho also offers workshops and events specifically for adults, such as science nights and maker workshops. These programs provide an opportunity for adults to engage with science in a social and relaxed setting.

c. School Programs and Field Trips

- **School Visits**: The Discovery Center of Idaho is a popular destination for school field trips, offering interactive exhibits and guided programs that align with educational standards. These visits provide students with hands-on experiences that reinforce classroom learning in a fun and engaging way.

- **Outreach Programs**: For schools that are unable to visit the center, DCI offers outreach programs where educators bring the excitement of science directly to the classroom. These programs include interactive demonstrations and hands-on activities that make science accessible to all students.

4. SPECIAL EVENTS AND COMMUNITY ENGAGEMENT

The Discovery Center of Idaho hosts a variety of special events throughout the year, many of which are designed to engage the community and promote science education.

a. Science with a Twist

- **Evening Events**: Science with a Twist is a series of evening events where adults can enjoy science in a more social setting. These events often feature themed activities, live demonstrations, and refreshments, making them a fun way to experience the center after hours.

b. First Friday Free Day

- **Free Admission**: On the first Friday of each month, the Discovery Center of Idaho offers free admission to all visitors. This community-focused event is a great way to explore the center's exhibits and participate in special activities at no cost.

c. Maker Faire

- **Celebrating Creativity and Innovation**: The Boise Mini Maker Faire, hosted by DCI, is an annual event that celebrates creativity, innovation, and the DIY spirit. The faire features exhibits, workshops, and demonstrations from local makers, inventors, and artists, providing inspiration and hands-on activities for visitors of all ages.

5. VISITING THE DISCOVERY CENTER OF IDAHO

Planning a visit to the Discovery Center of Idaho is easy, with a range of amenities and options to make your experience enjoyable.

a. Location and Hours

- **Central Location**: The Discovery Center of Idaho is conveniently located in downtown Boise, making it accessible for both locals and visitors. It's situated near other attractions like Julia Davis Park, the Boise River Greenbelt, and the Idaho State Museum, allowing you to easily explore multiple destinations in one day.

- **Operating Hours**: The center is open year-round, with hours varying depending on the season. Be sure to check the official website for the most up-to-date information on hours and any special closures.

b. Admission and Membership

- **Affordable Admission**: Admission prices are reasonable, with discounts available for children, seniors, students, and military personnel. The center also offers free admission on the first Friday of each month.

- **Membership Benefits**: If you plan to visit frequently, consider purchasing a membership. Membership provides unlimited access to the center for a year, as well as discounts on camps, workshops, and special events. Members also receive reciprocal admission to other science centers and museums across the country.

c. Amenities and Accessibility

- **Family-Friendly**: The Discovery Center of Idaho is designed with families in mind, offering stroller-friendly pathways, baby-changing stations, and seating areas for rest breaks. The center is also accessible to visitors with disabilities, ensuring that everyone can enjoy the exhibits and programs.

- **Gift Shop**: The on-site gift shop offers a variety of science-themed toys, books, and kits that allow visitors to continue their learning at home. It's a great place to pick up a souvenir or a unique gift for a budding scientist.

6. IMPACT ON THE COMMUNITY

The Discovery Center of Idaho plays a vital role in promoting STEM education and inspiring future generations of scientists, engineers, and innovators. Through its exhibits, programs, and community outreach, the center helps to foster a love of learning and a deeper understanding of the world around us. Its commitment to making science accessible to everyone, regardless of age or background, makes it a cornerstone of Boise's educational and cultural landscape.

5.3 JULIA DAVIS PARK: PLAYGROUNDS, MUSEUMS, AND MORE

Julia Davis Park is a central hub of recreation, culture, and relaxation in Boise. As one of the city's oldest and most beloved parks, it offers a wide range of activities and attractions for visitors of all ages. From sprawling playgrounds and scenic picnic areas to world-class museums and cultural institutions, Julia Davis Park has something for everyone. Here's a guide to the best of what Julia Davis Park has to offer.

1. OVERVIEW OF JULIA DAVIS PARK

Located along the Boise River and just a short walk from downtown Boise, Julia Davis Park is a 90-acre urban oasis that has been a cherished part of the city since it was donated by Thomas Jefferson Davis in 1907 in memory of his wife, Julia. The park is a key part of the Boise River Greenbelt and serves as a gathering place for both locals and visitors, offering a mix of natural beauty, recreational facilities, and cultural attractions.

2. PLAYGROUNDS AND FAMILY FUN

Julia Davis Park is a family-friendly destination, with several playgrounds and open spaces where children can play and explore.

a. Adventure Playground

- **Modern Play Area**: The Adventure Playground is a highlight for families visiting Julia Davis Park. This large, modern playground features a variety of play structures designed for children of all ages. Kids can enjoy climbing walls, slides, swings, and interactive play panels that encourage creativity and physical activity.

- **Shaded Areas and Seating**: The playground is surrounded by shaded areas and benches, making it a comfortable spot for parents to relax while keeping an eye on their children. The soft, rubberized surface ensures a safe play environment.

b. Open Spaces and Picnic Areas

- **Green Spaces**: The park's expansive lawns provide plenty of room for picnics, games, and relaxation. Families can spread out a blanket, enjoy a meal, and take in the beautiful surroundings. Many of the picnic areas are shaded by large trees, offering a cool retreat during the warmer months.

- **Picnic Shelters**: For larger gatherings, the park offers reservable picnic shelters equipped with tables and grills. These shelters are perfect for family reunions, birthday parties, or casual get-togethers.

c. Paddleboats and the Duck Pond

- **Paddleboats**: Julia Davis Park features a charming pond where visitors can rent paddleboats and enjoy a leisurely ride on the water. Paddleboating is a fun activity for families, couples, or friends, providing a unique way to experience the park from the water.

- **Duck Pond**: The Duck Pond is another popular attraction, especially for young children. Visitors can feed the ducks (with appropriate duck feed available at nearby stores), watch them swim, and enjoy the peaceful atmosphere of the pond.

3. MUSEUMS AND CULTURAL ATTRACTIONS

Julia Davis Park is home to several of Boise's most important cultural institutions, making it a cultural hub within the city.

a. Boise Art Museum (BAM)

- **Contemporary Art and More**: The Boise Art Museum, located within Julia Davis Park, offers a rich collection of contemporary art, with rotating exhibitions that showcase works from local, national, and international artists. The museum's permanent collection includes a variety of mediums, including painting, sculpture, photography, and mixed media.

- **Family Programs**: BAM regularly hosts family-friendly programs and workshops that encourage creative expression and art appreciation. These programs often include hands-on activities that allow visitors to explore their own artistic talents.

b. Idaho State Museum

- **Explore Idaho's History**: The Idaho State Museum provides an engaging look at the history, culture, and natural wonders of Idaho. With interactive exhibits, artifacts, and multimedia presentations, the museum covers everything from Idaho's Native American heritage to its role in the expansion of the American West.

- **Kid-Friendly Exhibits**: The museum features several exhibits designed specifically for children, including interactive displays that teach about Idaho's wildlife, geology, and history in a fun and accessible way.

c. Zoo Boise

- **Wildlife Encounters**: Located within Julia Davis Park, Zoo Boise is a top attraction for families and animal lovers. The zoo is home to over 300 animals from around the world, including giraffes, lions, red pandas, and more. Visitors can enjoy a variety of interactive experiences, such as feeding giraffes or taking a Conservation Cruise around the zoo's lagoon.

- **Educational Programs**: Zoo Boise offers educational programs for all ages, including camps, workshops, and guided tours that focus on wildlife conservation and environmental awareness.

d. Discovery Center of Idaho

- **Hands-On Science**: While technically located just outside the park, the Discovery Center of Idaho is a short walk away and is a must-visit for anyone interested in science and technology. The center offers over 200 interactive exhibits that explore topics such as physics, biology, and engineering. It's a place where visitors can engage with science through hands-on learning and experimentation.

4. GARDENS AND SCENIC AREAS

Julia Davis Park is not just a place for recreation; it's also a place to relax and enjoy the beauty of nature.

a. Rose Garden

- **A Romantic Retreat**: The Julia Davis Park Rose Garden is a beautifully landscaped area featuring over 2,000 rose bushes of various colors and varieties. The garden is a peaceful spot to stroll, relax, and enjoy the fragrance of blooming roses. It's also a popular location for weddings and special events.

- **Seasonal Beauty**: The best time to visit the Rose Garden is in late spring and early summer when the roses are in full bloom. The garden is meticulously maintained, providing a stunning display of floral beauty throughout the growing season.

b. Friendship Bridge

- **Connecting Park and University**: The Friendship Bridge is a pedestrian bridge that connects Julia Davis Park with the Boise State University campus across the Boise River. The bridge offers scenic views of the river and is a popular spot for walkers, joggers, and cyclists. It's also a great place to take photos, especially at sunset.

c. Boise River Greenbelt

- **Riverside Pathways**: The Boise River Greenbelt runs through Julia Davis Park, offering miles of scenic pathways along the Boise River. The Greenbelt is perfect for walking, jogging, cycling, or simply enjoying the natural beauty of the river. The pathways are lined with trees and provide access to several points of interest within the park.

5. SPECIAL EVENTS AND FESTIVALS

Julia Davis Park is a focal point for many of Boise's community events and festivals, bringing people together to celebrate arts, culture, and the outdoors.

a. Art in the Park

- **Annual Art Festival**: Every September, Julia Davis Park hosts Art in the Park, one of the largest and most popular art festivals in the region. The event features hundreds of artists and artisans from across the country, offering everything from paintings and sculptures to handmade jewelry and crafts. It's a vibrant celebration of creativity, with live music, food vendors, and interactive art activities for all ages.

b. Alive After Five

- **Summer Concert Series**: Alive After Five is a summer concert series held in downtown Boise, with many events taking place in or near Julia Davis Park. The series features live music from local and national artists, food trucks, and a festive atmosphere, making it a great way to enjoy a summer evening with family and friends.

c. Holiday Events

- **Seasonal Celebrations**: Julia Davis Park hosts a variety of holiday events throughout the year, including Easter egg hunts, Fourth of July celebrations, and winter holiday light displays. These events add a festive spirit to the park and provide opportunities for the community to come together and celebrate.

6. PLANNING YOUR VISIT

Julia Davis Park is open year-round, with different attractions and activities available depending on the season.

a. Accessibility

- **Easy Access**: The park is easily accessible from downtown Boise, with plenty of parking available in nearby lots. The park's pathways are paved and suitable for strollers and wheelchairs, making it accessible to all visitors.

- **Public Transportation**: For those who prefer not to drive, the park is well-served by Boise's public transportation system, with several bus routes stopping near the park's entrances.

b. Hours and Admission

- **Free Admission**: Admission to Julia Davis Park is free, although some attractions within the park, such as Zoo Boise and the museums, charge admission fees. Check the individual websites of these attractions for current pricing and hours of operation.

- **Peak Times**: The park can be busy during weekends, holidays, and special events, so plan accordingly if you prefer a quieter experience.

5.4 FAMILY-FRIENDLY DINING AND EVENTS

Boise is a city that embraces family life, offering a wide array of dining options and events that cater to both adults and children. Whether you're looking for a casual meal out with the kids, a special occasion spot, or fun events that the whole family can enjoy, Boise has plenty to offer. Here's a guide to some of the best family-friendly dining spots and events in the city.

1. FAMILY-FRIENDLY DINING IN BOISE

a. Big Jud's

- **What to Expect**: Big Jud's is a Boise institution known for its giant burgers and hearty portions. The casual, diner-style atmosphere is perfect for families, and the kids will love the fun challenge of trying to finish one of Big Jud's famously large burgers.

- **Menu Highlights**: Along with the signature Big Jud burger, the menu features kid-friendly options like grilled cheese, chicken strips, and milkshakes. The restaurant also offers vegetarian options and smaller portion sizes for little appetites.

- **Why It's Great for Families**: The laid-back atmosphere, friendly service, and impressive food make Big Jud's a hit with both kids and parents. It's a great spot for a casual family meal, and the kids will love seeing if they can conquer the giant burger challenge.

b. Flying Pie Pizzaria

- **What to Expect**: Flying Pie Pizzaria is a beloved Boise spot known for its creative pizzas and lively atmosphere. The restaurant is family-friendly, with plenty of space for kids to move around and a menu that appeals to all ages.

- **Menu Highlights**: The pizzas at Flying Pie are the star of the show, with options ranging from classic pepperoni to unique combinations like the "El Diablo" (spicy sausage, jalapeños, and crushed red pepper). Kids can also build their own pizzas, choosing from a variety of toppings.

- **Why It's Great for Families**: Flying Pie is a fun, casual spot where kids can enjoy watching their pizzas being made. The relaxed vibe and accommodating staff make it a great choice for families looking for a fun dining experience.

c. Westside Drive-In

- **What to Expect**: For a nostalgic dining experience, head to Westside Drive-In, a classic 1950s-style drive-in restaurant. Known for its comfort food and retro vibe, Westside is a hit with families who enjoy a bit of Americana with their meal.

- **Menu Highlights**: The menu includes diner favorites like burgers, hot dogs, milkshakes, and their famous "Idaho Ice Cream Potato" (a dessert made to look like a baked potato). There's also a selection of salads, sandwiches, and kids' meals.

- **Why It's Great for Families**: The drive-in experience is a novelty for kids, and the fun, retro atmosphere appeals to all ages. It's a great spot for a quick, affordable meal or a special treat like a milkshake or sundae.

d. The Matador

- **What to Expect**: The Matador is a family-friendly Mexican restaurant with a warm, welcoming atmosphere. The restaurant's vibrant décor and flavorful dishes make it a favorite for families who enjoy Mexican cuisine.

- **Menu Highlights**: The Matador offers a variety of Mexican dishes, including tacos, enchiladas, and burritos. There's also a kids' menu with smaller portions of kid-friendly options like quesadillas and chicken tenders. The restaurant is known for its fresh ingredients and house-made sauces.

- **Why It's Great for Families**: The Matador's lively atmosphere and diverse menu make it a great choice for families. Parents can enjoy a margarita while the kids dig into a plate of nachos or tacos. The restaurant is also accommodating to dietary restrictions, with plenty of gluten-free and vegetarian options.

e. Boise Fry Company

- **What to Expect**: Boise Fry Company is a casual eatery that specializes in gourmet fries and burgers. The restaurant's focus on quality ingredients and customizable options makes it a hit with both kids and adults.

- **Menu Highlights**: The fries at Boise Fry Company are the main attraction, with several varieties of potatoes and a wide range of dipping sauces to choose from. The burgers are made from grass-fed, free-range beef, and there are also veggie burger options for vegetarians. Kids will love picking their own fry variety and sauce combination.

- **Why It's Great for Families**: The casual, counter-service setup makes it easy for families to dine at their own pace. The focus on fries, a kid favorite, ensures that even picky eaters will find something they love. Plus, the restaurant's commitment to sustainability and locally sourced ingredients is a bonus for eco-conscious parents.

2. *FAMILY-FRIENDLY EVENTS IN BOISE*

a. Alive After Five

- **What to Expect**: Alive After Five is a free summer concert series held every Wednesday evening in downtown Boise. The event features live music from local and national artists, food vendors, and a lively, family-friendly atmosphere.

- **Why It's Great for Families**: Alive After Five is a great way for families to enjoy live music in a relaxed, outdoor setting. Kids can dance to the music, enjoy treats from the food trucks, and experience the vibrant energy of downtown Boise. The event is free, making it an affordable outing for the whole family.

b. Boise Farmer's Market

- **What to Expect**: The Boise Farmer's Market, held every Saturday from April through December, is a vibrant market featuring local produce, artisanal foods, and handmade goods. The market is a great place for families to explore, sample fresh foods, and learn about local agriculture.

- **Why It's Great for Families**: The market offers a wide variety of fresh, healthy foods that kids can sample, from fruits and vegetables to baked goods and cheeses. Many vendors offer kid-friendly activities, like face painting or crafts, making it a fun and educational experience for children.

c. Idaho Shakespeare Festival

- **What to Expect**: The Idaho Shakespeare Festival is a summer tradition in Boise, offering professional theater performances in an outdoor amphitheater. The festival features a mix of Shakespearean classics and contemporary plays, with something for everyone.

- **Why It's Great for Families**: The festival's relaxed, outdoor setting is perfect for families. Kids can enjoy the performances while sitting on the grass or in reserved seating. The festival also offers family nights with discounted tickets and special activities for children.

d. Zoo Boise's Boo at the Zoo

- **What to Expect**: Boo at the Zoo is Zoo Boise's annual Halloween event, where the zoo is transformed into a spook-tacular celebration with trick-or-treating, costume contests, and themed animal presentations.

- **Why It's Great for Families**: Boo at the Zoo is a safe and fun way for kids to enjoy Halloween. They can wear their costumes, collect treats, and learn about the zoo's animals in a festive atmosphere. The event is suitable for all ages, with activities that cater to both younger children and older kids.

e. Treefort Music Fest

- **What to Expect**: Treefort Music Fest is a multi-day music and arts festival held in downtown Boise every March. The festival features a diverse lineup of music, film, art, and storytelling events, with activities for all ages.

- **Why It's Great for Families**: Treefort offers Kidfort, a special section of the festival dedicated to children's activities. Kidfort includes family-friendly performances, workshops, and interactive art projects that allow kids to participate in the festival experience. The festival's inclusive atmosphere makes it a great outing for families looking to enjoy Boise's creative scene together.

f. Christmas in the City

- **What to Expect**: Christmas in the City is Boise's annual holiday celebration, featuring festive events throughout the downtown area. The event includes the lighting of the city's Christmas tree, holiday markets, caroling, and family-friendly activities.

- **Why It's Great for Families**: Christmas in the City is a magical way to kick off the holiday season with your family. Kids can visit with Santa, enjoy holiday treats, and take in the twinkling lights and festive decorations. The event also includes special performances and holiday-themed activities that are perfect for getting everyone in the holiday spirit.

Chapter 6: Boise's Natural Wonders

6.1 Boise National Forest: A Wilderness Escape

Nestled in the heart of Idaho, just a short drive from Boise, lies the sprawling Boise National Forest—a true wilderness escape that offers endless opportunities for adventure, relaxation, and immersion in nature. Covering over 2.5 million acres, the forest is a haven for outdoor enthusiasts, boasting rugged mountains, pristine rivers, dense forests, and abundant wildlife. Whether you're seeking a serene retreat or an adrenaline-pumping adventure, Boise National Forest has something for everyone. Here's a guide to discovering the best of what this incredible natural wonder has to offer.

1. Overview of Boise National Forest

Boise National Forest is part of the larger Sawtooth National Forest region and is one of Idaho's most cherished natural areas. The forest's diverse landscapes range from rolling foothills and alpine meadows to deep canyons and towering peaks. With its extensive network of trails, campgrounds, and waterways, the forest is a year-round destination for outdoor activities, including hiking, camping, fishing, and more.

The forest is divided into five ranger districts—Mountain Home, Idaho City, Lowman, Cascade, and Emmett—each offering unique attractions and experiences. The forest is also home to the North Fork of the Payette River, a world-renowned whitewater destination, as well as numerous hot springs, lakes, and scenic byways.

2. Hiking and Backpacking

Boise National Forest is a hiker's paradise, offering trails that range from easy day hikes to challenging multi-day backpacking adventures. With over 1,300 miles of trails, there's something for every level of hiker.

a. Baron Lakes Trail

- **Distance**: 12 miles (round trip)

- **Difficulty**: Moderate to Difficult

- **Highlights**: The Baron Lakes Trail is a stunning hike that takes you deep into the Sawtooth Wilderness. The trail winds through dense forests and along alpine ridges, offering breathtaking views of jagged peaks and pristine lakes. The highlight of the hike is the Baron Lakes themselves—three glacial lakes surrounded by granite cliffs and alpine meadows. This trail is popular with backpackers and offers excellent opportunities for fishing, photography, and solitude.

b. Rainbow Basin Trail

- **Distance**: 5 miles (round trip)

- **Difficulty**: Moderate

- **Highlights**: The Rainbow Basin Trail is a shorter hike that provides a wonderful mix of forested paths, open meadows, and scenic overlooks. The trail is known for its vibrant wildflowers in the spring and early summer, and the views of the surrounding mountains are spectacular. It's a great option for a half-day hike, with opportunities to spot wildlife such as deer, elk, and birds.

c. The Trinity Lakes Loop

- **Distance**: 8 miles (loop)

- **Difficulty**: Moderate

- **Highlights**: The Trinity Lakes Loop is a beautiful hike that takes you around several alpine lakes nestled in the Trinity Mountains. The trail is well-marked and offers stunning views of the lakes, mountains, and surrounding forest. The loop is a great option for both day hikers and those looking to camp overnight in a serene, lakeside setting.

d. Sawtooth Lake Trail

- **Distance**: 10 miles (round trip)

- **Difficulty**: Moderate

- **Highlights**: Sawtooth Lake is one of the most iconic destinations in the Sawtooth Wilderness, and the trail leading to it is equally impressive. The hike takes you through lush forests and past several smaller lakes before reaching the crystal-clear waters of Sawtooth Lake, surrounded by towering peaks. The trail is popular, especially in the summer, so plan to start early to enjoy some solitude at the lake.

3. CAMPING AND OVERNIGHT STAYS

Boise National Forest offers a variety of camping options, from developed campgrounds with amenities to remote backcountry sites for those seeking solitude.

a. Developed Campgrounds

- **Pine Flats Campground**: Located along the South Fork of the Payette River, Pine Flats is one of the most popular campgrounds in the forest. The campground offers tent and RV sites, with access to the river for fishing and swimming. A short hike from the campground leads to Pine Flats Hot Springs, where you can soak in natural hot pools surrounded by the forest.

- **Bull Trout Lake Campground**: Bull Trout Lake is a beautiful, high-altitude lake that offers excellent fishing, canoeing, and kayaking.

The campground is situated near the lake, with sites for tents and small RVs. The area is known for its peaceful atmosphere and stunning views of the surrounding mountains.

- **Warm Lake Campground**: Warm Lake is the largest natural lake in Boise National Forest, and the campground offers easy access to the water for swimming, boating, and fishing. The campground has tent and RV sites, as well as a boat launch and picnic areas. The nearby Warm Lake Lodge offers additional amenities, including a restaurant and rental cabins.

b. Dispersed Camping

For those seeking a more rugged experience, dispersed camping is allowed throughout much of Boise National Forest. Dispersed camping allows you to set up camp in undeveloped areas, away from established campgrounds. This option provides a true wilderness experience, with the opportunity to find your own secluded spot along a river, in a meadow, or near a mountain ridge.

c. Backcountry Camping

Backpacking and backcountry camping are popular in Boise National Forest, especially in the Sawtooth Wilderness. Permits are required for camping in some areas, and it's important to practice Leave No Trace principles to protect the pristine environment. Popular backcountry destinations include the Alice-Toxaway Loop, Sawtooth Lake, and the Baron Lakes.

4. FISHING AND BOATING

Boise National Forest is a haven for anglers and boaters, with numerous lakes, rivers, and streams offering excellent fishing opportunities. The forest is home to a variety of fish species, including rainbow trout, brook trout, cutthroat trout, and kokanee salmon.

a. Payette River

The Payette River is one of the premier fishing destinations in the forest, with its cold, clear waters supporting healthy populations of trout. The river offers both fly fishing and spin fishing opportunities, with sections ranging from gentle, meandering streams to fast-moving rapids. The North Fork of the Payette River is particularly popular with fly anglers, known for its challenging but rewarding fishing.

b. Deadwood Reservoir

Deadwood Reservoir is a large, high-altitude lake surrounded by the forest's rugged mountains. The reservoir is stocked with rainbow trout, kokanee salmon, and bull trout, making it a popular destination for fishing. The calm waters are also ideal for kayaking, canoeing, and paddleboarding. Several campgrounds are located near the reservoir, making it a great spot for a multi-day fishing trip.

c. Redfish Lake

While technically located just outside Boise National Forest, Redfish Lake is one of the most beautiful and popular destinations in the area. The lake is known for its crystal-clear waters and stunning mountain backdrop, making it a favorite spot for boating, fishing, and swimming. The lake is stocked with kokanee salmon and rainbow trout, and boat rentals are available at the Redfish Lake Lodge.

5. HOT SPRINGS

One of the unique features of Boise National Forest is its abundance of natural hot springs. These geothermal pools offer a relaxing way to soak and unwind after a day of hiking or exploring.

a. Pine Flats Hot Springs

Pine Flats Hot Springs is located near the Pine Flats Campground, along the South Fork of the Payette River. The hot springs feature a series of pools, some of which are perched above the river with stunning views of the surrounding forest. The springs are easily accessible by a short hike from the campground, making them a popular spot for campers and day visitors alike.

b. Kirkham Hot Springs

Kirkham Hot Springs is one of the most popular and accessible hot springs in Boise National Forest. Located along the South Fork of the Payette River, the springs feature several pools with varying temperatures, fed by natural geothermal water cascading over the rocks. The site includes a picnic area and changing facilities, making it a convenient stop for families and travelers.

c. Bonneville Hot Springs

Bonneville Hot Springs is a more remote and less crowded option, located off Highway 21 near the town of Lowman. The springs feature a series of rock-lined pools in a peaceful, forested setting. A short hike from the Bonneville Campground leads to the springs, which are popular with those seeking a more tranquil hot spring experience.

6. WILDLIFE WATCHING AND PHOTOGRAPHY

Boise National Forest is teeming with wildlife, making it a fantastic destination for wildlife watching and photography. The forest is home to a variety of species, including elk, deer, black bears, moose, and bald eagles.

a. Best Times and Places

- **Elk and Deer**: Elk and deer are commonly seen throughout the forest, especially in the early morning and late evening. The open meadows and river valleys near Cascade and Idaho City are prime spots for viewing these majestic animals.

- **Birdwatching**: The forest's diverse habitats support a wide range of bird species, including raptors, songbirds, and waterfowl. Bald eagles are often seen near large bodies of water like Deadwood

Reservoir and Warm Lake. The forest is also home to peregrine falcons, ospreys, and great blue herons.

- **Photographer's Paradise**: The varied landscapes of Boise National Forest offer endless opportunities for photography. From the rugged peaks and alpine lakes of the Sawtooth Wilderness to the tranquil rivers and hot springs, the forest provides stunning backdrops for capturing Idaho's natural beauty.

7. WINTER RECREATION

Boise National Forest is not just a summer destination—it's also a winter wonderland, offering activities like snowshoeing, cross-country skiing, snowmobiling, and even backcountry skiing.

a. Snowshoeing and Cross-Country Skiing

The forest's extensive trail system is perfect for winter sports enthusiasts. Snowshoeing and cross-country skiing are popular activities, with trails ranging from easy loops to challenging routes through the backcountry. Areas like the Trinity Mountains and the Cascade Ranger District offer excellent terrain and stunning winter scenery.

b. Snowmobiling

Boise National Forest is a top destination for snowmobiling, with hundreds of miles of groomed trails that wind through the forest's snowy landscapes. The Idaho City and Lowman Ranger Districts are particularly popular with snowmobilers, offering a mix of open meadows, forested trails, and mountain vistas.

c. Backcountry Skiing

For the more adventurous, backcountry skiing in the Sawtooth Wilderness offers an exhilarating way to explore the winter wilderness. The steep slopes and deep powder of the Sawtooth Mountains provide excellent conditions for experienced skiers looking to carve their own path through the snow.

8. SCENIC DRIVES

If you prefer to explore the forest by car, several scenic byways and drives offer breathtaking views and access to many of the forest's highlights.

a. Ponderosa Pine Scenic Byway

The Ponderosa Pine Scenic Byway (Highway 21) is a stunning drive that takes you through the heart of Boise National Forest. The byway stretches from Boise to Stanley, passing through charming towns like Idaho City and Lowman. Along the way, you'll encounter towering pines, rushing rivers, and majestic mountain vistas. Highlights include Kirkham Hot Springs, the Payette River, and views of the Sawtooth Mountains.

b. Wildlife Canyon Scenic Byway

The Wildlife Canyon Scenic Byway (Highway 55 and Banks-Lowman Road) offers a picturesque journey along the South Fork of the Payette River. The byway is known for its abundant wildlife, including elk, deer, and bald eagles, making it a perfect route for wildlife enthusiasts. The road winds through deep canyons and lush forests, offering numerous pull-offs for scenic views and photo opportunities.

c. Sawtooth Scenic Byway

The Sawtooth Scenic Byway (Highway 75) takes you through some of the most breathtaking landscapes in Idaho, including the Sawtooth Wilderness and Redfish Lake. While part of this byway lies outside Boise National Forest, it's an easy day trip from the forest and offers incredible views of the Sawtooth Mountains, pristine lakes, and alpine meadows. The byway also passes through the historic town of Stanley, a gateway to the Sawtooth National Recreation Area.

6.2 Idaho Botanical Garden: Plants and Seasonal Displays

The Idaho Botanical Garden (IBG) is a serene and beautiful destination in Boise, offering visitors a chance to explore an array of plants, gardens, and seasonal displays that celebrate the natural beauty of Idaho and the Intermountain West. Nestled in the foothills of the Boise Mountains, the garden is a year-round haven for plant lovers, nature enthusiasts, and anyone seeking a peaceful retreat in a picturesque setting. Here's an in-depth look at what the Idaho Botanical Garden has to offer.

1. Overview of the Idaho Botanical Garden

The Idaho Botanical Garden is situated on 50 acres of land that was once part of the Old Idaho Penitentiary, providing a unique historical backdrop to the gardens. Since its founding in 1984, the garden has grown into a vibrant space that showcases a diverse collection of plants adapted to the local climate, along with themed gardens, educational exhibits, and special events.

The garden's mission is to promote an understanding of plants, gardening, and conservation through its displays, programs, and outreach efforts. It serves as both a living museum and an educational resource, drawing visitors from Boise and beyond to experience the beauty and diversity of plant life.

2. Themed Gardens and Plant Collections

The Idaho Botanical Garden features several themed gardens and plant collections, each designed to highlight specific plant types, gardening styles, or ecological concepts. These gardens provide a rich tapestry of colors, textures, and scents, offering something new to discover with each visit.

a. English Garden

- **Classic Design**: The English Garden is a formal garden inspired by traditional English landscaping. It features neatly trimmed hedges, vibrant flower beds, and a charming gazebo. The garden is designed to evoke the elegance and symmetry of English gardens, with seasonal displays of roses, tulips, and other classic flowers.

- **Relaxing Atmosphere**: With its winding paths and shaded benches, the English Garden is a perfect spot for a quiet stroll or a peaceful moment of reflection. It's also a popular location for weddings and other special events.

b. Rose Garden

- **Aromatic Beauty**: The Rose Garden is a fragrant haven filled with a stunning variety of roses. From classic hybrid teas to hardy shrub roses, the garden showcases a wide range of colors and forms. The roses are meticulously cared for, ensuring a spectacular display from late spring through early fall.

- **Educational Aspect**: The Rose Garden also serves as an educational resource, with information about rose care, pruning techniques, and disease management available to visitors. It's a great place to learn more about cultivating roses in your own garden.

c. Water Conservation Landscape

- **Sustainable Gardening**: The Water Conservation Landscape demonstrates how to create beautiful, low-water-use gardens in the arid climate of the Intermountain West. The garden features drought-tolerant plants, including native species, ornamental grasses, and succulents, arranged in attractive, water-wise designs.

- **Inspiration for Home Gardens**: This garden provides practical ideas for homeowners looking to reduce their water usage while still maintaining a vibrant and diverse landscape. It's a valuable resource for anyone interested in sustainable gardening practices.

d. Meditation Garden

- **Peaceful Retreat**: The Meditation Garden is designed as a tranquil space for contemplation and relaxation. The garden features a variety of plants known for their calming effects, along with water features, secluded seating areas, and shaded walkways.

- **Spiritual Elements**: Inspired by Japanese and Zen gardens, the Meditation Garden includes symbolic elements such as stones, bamboo, and water, creating a serene environment that encourages mindfulness and inner peace.

e. Idaho Native Plant Garden

- **Celebrating Native Flora**: The Idaho Native Plant Garden showcases the rich diversity of Idaho's native plants, including wildflowers, shrubs, and grasses. This garden emphasizes the importance of preserving native species and habitats, and it provides visitors with a deeper understanding of the plants that thrive in Idaho's unique ecosystems.

- **Seasonal Displays**: The garden is particularly beautiful in the spring and early summer, when native wildflowers like lupines, penstemons, and paintbrushes are in full bloom. Interpretive signs offer information about each plant species and its role in the local environment.

f. Lewis & Clark Native Plant Garden

- **Historical Exploration**: This garden is inspired by the plants documented by the Lewis and Clark Expedition as they traveled through the Pacific Northwest. The garden features species that were collected and recorded during the expedition, offering a historical perspective on the region's flora.

- **Educational Focus**: The Lewis & Clark Native Plant Garden includes interpretive displays that highlight the historical significance of the plants, as well as their traditional uses by Native

American tribes. It's an educational experience that connects botany with history.

g. Vegetable Garden

- **Urban Agriculture**: The Vegetable Garden is a productive space where visitors can learn about growing their own food. The garden features raised beds filled with a variety of vegetables, herbs, and edible flowers. It's a great resource for those interested in urban gardening or sustainable agriculture.

- **Seasonal Harvests**: Throughout the growing season, the Vegetable Garden offers demonstrations and workshops on topics such as composting, crop rotation, and organic pest control. Visitors can see firsthand how to grow and harvest fresh produce in a small space.

h. Children's Adventure Garden

- **Interactive Learning**: The Children's Adventure Garden is a playful, interactive space designed to engage young visitors in hands-on learning about plants and the natural world. The garden features themed areas such as a butterfly garden, a sensory garden, and a discovery station where kids can dig, plant, and explore.

- **Family Fun**: With its vibrant colors, whimsical designs, and educational exhibits, the Children's Adventure Garden is a favorite spot for families. It encourages curiosity and creativity while teaching important lessons about nature and gardening.

3. SEASONAL DISPLAYS AND EVENTS

The Idaho Botanical Garden is a year-round destination, with each season bringing new displays, events, and activities that showcase the garden's beauty and diversity.

a. Spring Bloom

- **Explosions of Color**: Spring is one of the most beautiful times to visit the Idaho Botanical Garden, as the entire garden comes to life with a riot of colors. Tulips, daffodils, magnolias, and other spring bulbs create stunning displays throughout the garden. The Rose Garden and English Garden are particularly vibrant during this time.

- **Spring Events**: The garden hosts a variety of spring events, including guided tours, gardening workshops, and plant sales. These events offer visitors a chance to learn more about spring gardening and to purchase plants for their own gardens.

b. Summer Splendor

- **Peak Bloom**: Summer is the season of peak bloom at the Idaho Botanical Garden, with roses, perennials, and annuals all reaching their full glory. The garden's shaded paths, water features, and colorful displays make it a perfect spot to escape the heat and enjoy the outdoors.

- **Great Garden Escape Concert Series**: One of the highlights of summer at the garden is the Great Garden Escape Concert Series. This popular event features live music in the garden's beautiful setting, with performances from local and regional artists. Visitors can bring a picnic, relax on the lawn, and enjoy an evening of music under the stars.

c. Fall Harvest Festival

- **Autumn Colors**: As the seasons change, the garden takes on the warm hues of autumn. Fall is a great time to see the garden's trees and shrubs in their fall colors, as well as to enjoy the late-blooming perennials and ornamental grasses.

- **Harvest Festival**: The Fall Harvest Festival is a family-friendly event that celebrates the bounty of the garden. Activities include pumpkin carving, apple pressing, and garden-themed crafts for kids. It's a fun and festive way to enjoy the season and learn about fall gardening.

d. Winter Garden aGlow

- **Holiday Magic**: During the holiday season, the Idaho Botanical Garden is transformed into a winter wonderland with the Winter Garden aGlow event. Thousands of twinkling lights, festive displays, and holiday music create a magical atmosphere that's perfect for families and visitors of all ages.

- **Special Activities**: In addition to the stunning light displays, Winter Garden aGlow features visits from Santa, holiday treats, and warm beverages. The event is a beloved Boise tradition and a must-see during the holiday season.

4. EDUCATIONAL PROGRAMS AND WORKSHOPS

The Idaho Botanical Garden is dedicated to education and offers a variety of programs, workshops, and classes for gardeners of all levels.

a. Gardening Workshops

- **Practical Learning**: The garden offers workshops throughout the year on topics such as pruning, composting, water-wise gardening, and native plant landscaping. These workshops provide practical, hands-on learning experiences that help participants develop their gardening skills.

- **Expert Instruction**: Workshops are led by experienced gardeners, horticulturists, and botanists who share their knowledge and tips for success. Whether you're a novice gardener or an experienced green thumb, there's always something new to learn.

b. Plant Sales

- **Seasonal Sales**: The garden hosts seasonal plant sales in the spring and fall, offering a wide selection of plants that are well-suited to

Idaho's climate. The sales feature native plants, perennials, shrubs, trees, and more, with knowledgeable staff on hand to provide advice on plant selection and care.

- **Supporting the Garden**: Proceeds from plant sales help support the garden's programs and maintenance, making it a great way to enhance your own garden while contributing to a good cause.

c. Children's Education Programs

- **Youth Engagement**: The Idaho Botanical Garden offers a range of educational programs for children, including school field trips, summer camps, and family workshops. These programs are designed to inspire a love of nature and gardening in young people, with hands-on activities that make learning fun.

- **Junior Master Gardener Program**: The Junior Master Gardener Program is a special initiative that provides in-depth gardening education for children. Participants learn about plant science, ecology, and conservation through a series of engaging lessons and projects.

5. *MEMBERSHIP AND VISITOR INFORMATION*

Becoming a member of the Idaho Botanical Garden is a great way to support the garden while enjoying a range of benefits.

a. Membership Benefits

- **Unlimited Access**: Members receive unlimited access to the garden throughout the year, including special members-only events and early admission to plant sales.

- **Discounts and Perks**: Membership also includes discounts on workshops, classes, and event tickets, as well as a 10% discount at the garden's gift shop. Members also receive a subscription to the garden's newsletter, which provides updates on upcoming events, plant care tips, and more.

b. Planning Your Visit

- **Hours and Admission**: The garden is open year-round, with hours varying by season. Admission fees are reasonable, with discounts available for seniors, students, and children. Memberships offer additional savings and benefits.

- **Accessibility**: The Idaho Botanical Garden is fully accessible, with paved paths and ramps that make it easy for visitors of all abilities to explore the gardens. Wheelchairs are available for loan at the visitor center.

6.3 LUCKY PEAK STATE PARK: BOATING, FISHING, AND PICNICKING

Lucky Peak State Park, located just a short drive from downtown Boise, is a popular destination for outdoor enthusiasts looking to enjoy the beauty of Idaho's natural landscapes. The park is known for its wide range of recreational activities, particularly boating, fishing, and picnicking, making it an ideal spot for families, groups of friends, and anyone seeking a day of fun and relaxation in the great outdoors. Here's a guide to making the most of your visit to Lucky Peak State Park.

1. OVERVIEW OF LUCKY PEAK STATE PARK

Lucky Peak State Park is situated along the Boise River and is centered around the Lucky Peak Reservoir, a large body of water that provides opportunities for a variety of water-based activities. The park is divided into three main areas: Discovery Park, Sandy Point, and Spring Shores, each offering its own unique attractions and amenities.

- **Discovery Park**: A popular spot for picnicking and family gatherings, Discovery Park features lush green lawns, shaded picnic areas, and easy access to the Boise River.

- **Sandy Point**: Located at the base of the Lucky Peak Dam, Sandy Point is a favorite spot for swimming and beach activities, with a sandy shoreline and calm waters perfect for a day of sun and fun.

- **Spring Shores**: This area serves as the hub for boating activities, with a marina, boat ramps, and rentals available for those looking to explore the reservoir by water.

2. BOATING AT LUCKY PEAK RESERVOIR

Lucky Peak Reservoir is a haven for boating enthusiasts, offering a large expanse of water surrounded by scenic hills and rugged landscapes. Whether you're into powerboating, sailing, kayaking, or paddleboarding, Lucky Peak has something for everyone.

a. Powerboating and Watersports

- **Open Waters**: The wide-open waters of the reservoir are perfect for powerboating, water skiing, wakeboarding, and tubing. The large size of the reservoir means there's plenty of room to spread out and enjoy your favorite watersports without feeling crowded.

- **Marina Services**: The Spring Shores Marina offers boat rentals, fuel, and supplies, making it easy to get out on the water even if you don't own a boat. The marina also provides boat slips and mooring facilities for those who prefer to bring their own watercraft.

b. Sailing and Kayaking

- **Sailing Adventures**: The steady winds and expansive water surface make Lucky Peak Reservoir an excellent destination for sailing. Sailboats of various sizes can be seen gliding across the reservoir, taking advantage of the favorable conditions.

- **Kayaking and Paddleboarding**: For a quieter, more leisurely experience, kayaking and paddleboarding are great ways to explore the shoreline and coves of the reservoir. The calm waters near the shore are ideal for beginners and those looking to enjoy a peaceful paddle surrounded by nature.

c. Boat Ramps and Launches

- **Convenient Access**: Spring Shores is the primary location for boat launching, with multiple ramps available to accommodate a variety of watercraft. The ramps are well-maintained and provide easy access to the water, ensuring a smooth start to your boating adventure.

- **Boat Rentals**: If you don't have your own boat, the marina offers a range of rental options, including motorboats, pontoon boats, and personal watercraft like jet skis. Rentals are available by the hour or for the full day, allowing you to customize your time on the water.

3. FISHING AT LUCKY PEAK

Lucky Peak Reservoir is also a popular fishing destination, offering excellent opportunities to catch a variety of fish species. The reservoir is regularly stocked with trout, and the surrounding waters are home to several other fish species, making it a great spot for anglers of all skill levels.

a. Fish Species

- **Trout**: Rainbow trout are the most common catch at Lucky Peak, with the Idaho Department of Fish and Game regularly stocking the reservoir to ensure a healthy population. These fish are most active in the cooler months, but can be caught year-round.

- **Kokanee Salmon**: The reservoir also supports a population of kokanee salmon, a landlocked version of the sockeye salmon. Kokanee are known for their fight and are a prized catch among local anglers.

- **Smallmouth Bass**: Smallmouth bass can be found in the warmer, shallow areas of the reservoir, particularly during the summer months. These fish are known for their aggressive strikes and are a favorite among sport fishers.

b. Best Fishing Spots

- **Near the Dam**: The area near the Lucky Peak Dam is one of the most popular fishing spots, particularly for trout. The deep, cool waters provide an ideal habitat for these fish, and the rocky structure near the dam offers good cover for bass and other species.

- **Shoreline and Coves**: The coves and inlets along the shoreline of the reservoir are also great places to fish, especially for those looking to catch bass or sunfish. These areas offer calmer waters and plenty of structure for fish to hide, making them ideal for shore fishing or fishing from a small boat or kayak.

c. Fishing Tips

- **Early Morning and Late Evening**: The best times to fish at Lucky Peak are typically early in the morning or late in the evening when the fish are most active. During these times, the water is cooler, and the fish are more likely to be feeding near the surface.

- **Trolling**: Trolling is a popular technique for catching trout and kokanee in the deeper waters of the reservoir. Using lures or bait that mimics the fish's natural prey can be particularly effective.

4. PICNICKING AND FAMILY FUN

Lucky Peak State Park is an ideal spot for a family picnic, offering beautiful scenery, well-maintained facilities, and plenty of space for relaxation and play.

a. Picnic Areas

- **Discovery Park**: This area is the most popular for picnicking, with large, grassy fields, shaded picnic tables, and barbecue grills available for use. The park's proximity to the Boise River makes it a scenic spot to enjoy a meal while taking in views of the water and surrounding mountains.

- **Sandy Point**: If you're looking for a picnic spot closer to the water, Sandy Point is a great choice. The area features picnic tables along the beach, allowing you to enjoy your meal with your toes in the sand and the sound of the water nearby.

b. Playground and Swimming

- **Sandy Point Beach**: Sandy Point is the park's designated swimming area, offering a sandy beach and calm, shallow waters that are perfect for families with young children. The beach is a great place to build sandcastles, swim, or simply relax in the sun.

- **Playground Facilities**: Discovery Park features a playground with slides, swings, and climbing structures, providing plenty of entertainment for kids. The open grassy areas are also ideal for playing frisbee, soccer, or other outdoor games.

c. Group Shelters and Events

- **Group Shelters**: For larger gatherings, Lucky Peak State Park offers reservable group shelters equipped with tables, grills, and nearby restrooms. These shelters are perfect for family reunions, birthday parties, or corporate events.

- **Special Events**: The park hosts a variety of events throughout the year, including outdoor concerts, fishing derbies, and holiday celebrations. Check the park's calendar for upcoming events that you can enjoy with family and friends.

5. *HIKING AND EXPLORING THE SURROUNDINGS*

In addition to water-based activities, Lucky Peak State Park offers several hiking trails that allow visitors to explore the natural beauty of the area.

a. Lucky Peak Trail

- **Trail Details**: The Lucky Peak Trail is a moderate to challenging hike that takes you to the top of Lucky Peak, offering stunning views of the Boise River, the reservoir, and the surrounding foothills. The trail is approximately 13 miles round trip and gains about 3,000 feet in elevation.

- **Why Hike It**: The trail is well-maintained and offers a rewarding hike with panoramic views at the summit. It's a great option for those looking to combine a day of boating or fishing with a scenic hike.

b. Boise River Greenbelt

- **Trail Details**: The Boise River Greenbelt is a paved trail that runs along the Boise River, connecting various parks and natural areas, including Lucky Peak. The Greenbelt is perfect for walking, jogging, cycling, or simply enjoying a leisurely stroll along the river.

- **Why Hike It**: The Greenbelt offers easy access to the park's natural beauty and provides a peaceful setting for a walk or bike ride. The trail is also family-friendly, making it a great option for visitors of all ages.

6. PLANNING YOUR VISIT

Lucky Peak State Park is open year-round, with different activities available depending on the season.

a. Best Times to Visit

- **Summer**: The summer months are the most popular time to visit Lucky Peak, as the warm weather makes it ideal for boating, fishing, swimming, and picnicking. The park can get busy on weekends, so plan to arrive early if you want to secure a good spot.

- **Fall and Spring**: These seasons offer cooler temperatures and fewer crowds, making them a great time for hiking, fishing, and enjoying the park's natural beauty. The fall foliage adds a beautiful touch to the landscape, and the spring wildflowers are a delight to see.

b. Fees and Permits

- **Day-Use Fees**: A small entrance fee is required for day use of the park, which helps maintain the facilities and services. Annual passes are also available for frequent visitors.

- **Boating Permits**: If you plan to bring your own boat, make sure you have the necessary permits, including invasive species stickers, which are required for all watercraft in Idaho.

c. Amenities and Accessibility

- **Facilities**: The park offers a range of amenities, including restrooms, picnic areas, playgrounds, and a marina. The facilities are well-maintained and easily accessible.

- **Accessibility**: Lucky Peak State Park is accessible to visitors of all abilities, with paved paths, wheelchair-accessible restrooms, and designated parking areas.

6.4 DEER FLAT NATIONAL WILDLIFE REFUGE: BIRDWATCHING AND TRAILS

Deer Flat National Wildlife Refuge, located near Nampa, Idaho, is a serene and scenic destination that offers exceptional opportunities for birdwatching and hiking. Established in 1909, the refuge is one of the oldest in the National Wildlife Refuge System and serves as a critical habitat for a diverse array of wildlife, particularly migratory birds. With its combination of wetlands, grasslands, and upland areas, Deer Flat is a must-visit location for nature enthusiasts and anyone seeking to connect with the natural world.

1. OVERVIEW OF DEER FLAT NATIONAL WILDLIFE REFUGE

Deer Flat National Wildlife Refuge encompasses over 11,000 acres and includes two distinct units: the Lake Lowell Unit and the Snake River Islands Unit. The Lake Lowell Unit, centered around the 9,000-acre Lake Lowell, is the most accessible and popular area for visitors. The Snake River Islands Unit consists of over 100 islands scattered along the Snake River, providing additional habitat for wildlife and unique opportunities for exploration.

The refuge plays a vital role in the conservation of migratory birds, offering nesting, feeding, and resting areas for a wide variety of species. It's also a great place for hiking, wildlife observation, and photography, with trails and viewing areas that allow visitors to experience the refuge's natural beauty up close.

2. BIRDWATCHING AT DEER FLAT NATIONAL WILDLIFE REFUGE

Deer Flat is renowned for its birdwatching opportunities, attracting birders from all over the region. The refuge is home to more than 200 species of birds, making it a year-round haven for birdwatching enthusiasts.

a. Migratory Birds

- **Waterfowl**: During the fall and winter months, Lake Lowell becomes a critical stopover for thousands of migratory waterfowl, including mallards, northern pintails, Canada geese, and tundra swans. The lake's calm waters and abundant food supply make it an ideal location for these birds to rest and refuel during their long migrations.

- **Shorebirds**: In the spring and early summer, the refuge's wetlands and mudflats attract a variety of shorebirds, such as sandpipers, plovers, and avocets. These birds can often be seen probing the mud for insects and other invertebrates, providing great opportunities for observation and photography.

- **Songbirds**: The refuge's diverse habitats, including forests, grasslands, and wetlands, support a wide range of songbirds throughout the year. Species such as western meadowlarks, yellow warblers, and black-headed grosbeaks are common sights, especially during the breeding season.

b. Raptors

- **Eagles and Hawks**: Deer Flat is also a prime location for spotting raptors, including bald eagles, ospreys, and red-tailed hawks. Bald eagles are particularly abundant in the winter, when they can often be seen perched in trees around the lake or soaring overhead in search of fish.

- **Owls**: The refuge is home to several species of owls, including great horned owls and barn owls. These nocturnal hunters are most active at dawn and dusk, making them a special treat for birdwatchers who visit during these times.

c. Birdwatching Tips

- **Best Times to Visit**: The best times for birdwatching at Deer Flat are during the early morning and late afternoon, when birds are most active. The fall and spring migrations offer particularly rewarding experiences, with large numbers of birds passing through the area.

- **Bring Binoculars and a Field Guide**: To fully enjoy the birdwatching experience, bring a good pair of binoculars and a field guide to help identify the different species you encounter. The refuge also offers bird checklists and brochures to assist with identification.

- **Respect Wildlife and Stay on Trails**: While birdwatching, it's important to respect the wildlife and their habitats by staying on designated trails and maintaining a safe distance from the birds. This helps ensure that the birds are not disturbed and can continue to thrive in their natural environment.

3. HIKING AND TRAILS AT DEER FLAT NATIONAL WILDLIFE REFUGE

Deer Flat offers a variety of trails that allow visitors to explore the refuge's diverse landscapes, from lakeshore paths to upland hikes. These trails are perfect for casual walkers, serious hikers, and anyone looking to immerse themselves in nature.

a. The Lakeshore Trail

- **Trail Overview**: The Lakeshore Trail is a popular, easy-to-moderate trail that winds along the northern shore of Lake Lowell. The trail offers beautiful views of the lake and the surrounding wetlands, with plenty of opportunities to spot waterfowl, shorebirds, and other wildlife.

- **Distance and Difficulty**: The trail is approximately 5 miles long (round trip) and relatively flat, making it suitable for hikers of all ages and skill levels. The well-maintained path is also accessible for strollers and wheelchairs in some sections.

- **What to See**: In addition to birdwatching, the Lakeshore Trail offers scenic views of the lake, wildflowers in the spring, and stunning fall foliage. Interpretive signs along the trail provide information about the refuge's history, wildlife, and conservation efforts.

b. The Kingfisher Trail

- **Trail Overview**: The Kingfisher Trail is a shorter, more accessible trail that loops through a section of riparian forest near the Visitor

Center. This easy trail is perfect for families and those looking for a shorter walk.

- **Distance and Difficulty**: The Kingfisher Trail is a 1.2-mile loop with minimal elevation gain. The trail is well-marked and mostly shaded, making it a pleasant walk even on warmer days.

- **What to See**: This trail is an excellent spot for observing songbirds, woodpeckers, and other forest-dwelling species. The trail's proximity to the Visitor Center also makes it a convenient option for a quick nature walk.

c. The Observation Hill Trail

- **Trail Overview**: The Observation Hill Trail offers a more challenging hike with rewarding views of the refuge and the surrounding landscape. The trail leads to the top of a small hill, where a viewing platform provides panoramic vistas of Lake Lowell and the Boise Mountains.

- **Distance and Difficulty**: The trail is a 2-mile loop with a moderate incline, making it a good choice for those looking for a bit of a workout. The trail is less crowded than some of the other options, offering a more peaceful hiking experience.

- **What to See**: From the top of Observation Hill, you'll have a bird's-eye view of the refuge, making it an excellent spot for spotting eagles, hawks, and other birds of prey. The trail also passes through a mix of habitats, including grasslands and sagebrush, providing opportunities to see a variety of plant and animal species.

d. The Nature Center and Short Interpretive Trails

- **Visitor Center and Exhibits**: The refuge's Visitor Center offers educational exhibits, maps, and information about the refuge's wildlife and history. It's a great starting point for your visit, providing context and background for what you'll see on the trails.

- **Short Interpretive Trails**: Near the Visitor Center, you'll find several short, interpretive trails that provide a closer look at specific habitats and species. These trails are designed to be informative and engaging, making them a great option for families and those new to the refuge.

4. WILDLIFE WATCHING BEYOND BIRDS

While Deer Flat is best known for its birdwatching, the refuge is also home to a wide range of other wildlife, making it a great destination for nature enthusiasts of all kinds.

a. Mammals

- **White-tailed Deer**: As the name suggests, Deer Flat is a great place to spot white-tailed deer, especially in the early morning or late evening. These graceful animals are often seen grazing in the meadows or moving quietly through the forests.

- **Coyotes and Foxes**: The refuge's diverse habitats support populations of coyotes and red foxes. These elusive predators are most active at dawn and dusk, and their tracks can often be seen along the trails.

- **Beavers and Muskrats**: The wetlands and waterways of Deer Flat are home to beavers and muskrats, which can be seen swimming in the lakes and streams or working on their lodges and dams. Look for signs of their activity, such as chewed tree trunks and mud slides.

b. Reptiles and Amphibians

- **Western Painted Turtles**: The wetlands and ponds around Lake Lowell are home to Western painted turtles, which can often be seen basking on logs or rocks. These colorful turtles are a favorite sight for visitors, especially on sunny days.

- **Frogs and Salamanders**: The refuge's wetlands are also home to a variety of amphibians, including frogs and salamanders. These creatures are more commonly heard than seen, but with a bit of patience, you may spot them near the water's edge.

c. Insects and Pollinators

- **Butterflies and Bees**: The refuge's wildflower meadows attract a variety of pollinators, including butterflies, bees, and hummingbirds. These species play a vital role in the ecosystem, and their presence adds to the diversity and beauty of the refuge.

- **Dragonflies and Damselflies**: The wetlands are also home to numerous dragonflies and damselflies, which can be seen darting over the water in search of prey. These agile insects are fascinating to watch and are an important part of the refuge's food web.

5. *Planning Your Visit*

Deer Flat National Wildlife Refuge is open year-round, with different activities and wildlife viewing opportunities available depending on the season.

a. Best Times to Visit

- **Spring and Fall**: These seasons offer the best birdwatching opportunities, with migratory birds passing through the refuge in large numbers. The mild weather and vibrant colors of the landscape also make these ideal times for hiking and photography.

- **Winter**: Winter is a great time to visit if you're interested in seeing bald eagles and other raptors, which are more abundant during this time. The refuge is also quieter in the winter, offering a peaceful retreat for those looking to escape the crowds.

- **Summer**: While summer can be hot, it's a good time for early morning or evening hikes. The wildflowers are in bloom, and the refuge's wetlands are teeming with life, making it a rewarding time to explore.

b. Accessibility and Amenities

- **Visitor Center**: The Visitor Center is open year-round and offers educational exhibits, maps, and restrooms. It's a great place to start your visit and get oriented to the refuge.

- **Parking and Trail Access**: Parking is available at several trailheads and the Visitor Center. The trails are well-marked, and most are accessible for visitors of all abilities.

- **Permits and Fees**: There is no entrance fee for Deer Flat National Wildlife Refuge, making it an affordable destination for outdoor recreation. However, certain activities, such as fishing, may require permits.

c. Safety and Etiquette

- **Wildlife Safety**: While exploring the refuge, it's important to respect the wildlife and maintain a safe distance from animals, especially larger mammals like deer and coyotes. Avoid feeding the wildlife and stay on designated trails to protect both yourself and the environment.

- **Leave No Trace**: Practice Leave No Trace principles by packing out all trash, staying on trails, and minimizing your impact on the natural environment. This helps preserve the beauty and integrity of the refuge for future generations.

CHAPTER 7: LOCAL CUISINE AND DINING

7.1 FARM-TO-TABLE DINING: FRESH, LOCAL FLAVORS

Boise has embraced the farm-to-table dining movement with enthusiasm, making it a top destination for food lovers seeking fresh, locally sourced ingredients and innovative culinary experiences. The farm-to-table philosophy emphasizes the use of seasonal produce, meats, and other ingredients that are grown and harvested locally, often within a short distance of the restaurant. This approach not only supports local farmers and producers but also ensures that the food on your plate is as fresh and flavorful as possible. Here's a guide to some of the best farm-to-table dining experiences in Boise, where you can savor the true taste of Idaho.

1. THE ESSENCE OF FARM-TO-TABLE DINING

Farm-to-table dining is more than just a trend—it's a commitment to sustainability, quality, and community. By sourcing ingredients from nearby farms, ranches, and artisanal producers, restaurants in Boise are able to offer dishes that reflect the unique flavors of the region. Seasonal menus, which change throughout the year based on what's fresh and available, allow chefs to be creative and offer diners a constantly evolving culinary experience.

a. Supporting Local Agriculture

- **Direct Sourcing**: Farm-to-table restaurants often establish direct relationships with local farmers, ranchers, and food artisans. This not only guarantees freshness but also supports the local economy and promotes sustainable agricultural practices.

- **Seasonal Menus**: Because farm-to-table dining is based on what's in season, menus at these restaurants change regularly. This means that no two visits are ever the same, and diners get to experience the best of what the region has to offer at any given time.

b. Sustainability and Quality

- **Eco-Friendly Practices**: Many farm-to-table restaurants prioritize sustainability in every aspect of their operations, from using organic and non-GMO ingredients to reducing waste and conserving energy. This commitment to the environment resonates with diners who are mindful of their food choices.

- **Unmatched Freshness**: With ingredients often harvested just hours before they reach the kitchen, farm-to-table dining offers an unparalleled level of freshness. This results in dishes that are vibrant, flavorful, and reflective of the natural beauty of Idaho's landscape.

2. TOP FARM-TO-TABLE RESTAURANTS IN BOISE

Boise is home to a growing number of farm-to-table restaurants, each offering its own unique take on local cuisine. Here are some of the standout spots where you can enjoy fresh, local flavors:

a. The Modern Hotel and Bar

- **Overview**: The Modern Hotel and Bar is a chic, urban spot that has gained a reputation for its innovative farm-to-table cuisine. Located in the Linen District, The Modern offers a menu that changes with the seasons, highlighting the best of Idaho's local produce, meats, and artisanal products.

- **Menu Highlights**: The Modern's menu features dishes like smoked trout salad with seasonal greens, local beef tartare, and house-made pastas with farm-fresh vegetables. The bar also serves craft cocktails made with locally distilled spirits and house-infused syrups, making it a great place to relax and enjoy Boise's culinary scene.

- **Why It's Special**: The Modern is known for its creativity and attention to detail, both in its food and its presentation. The minimalist, stylish atmosphere adds to the dining experience, making it a favorite for both locals and visitors.

b. Bittercreek Alehouse

- **Overview**: Bittercreek Alehouse is a downtown Boise institution that has been committed to sustainable, farm-to-table dining for years. The restaurant partners with local farmers and producers to create a menu that is both delicious and environmentally conscious.

- **Menu Highlights**: Known for its extensive selection of local beers on tap, Bittercreek's food menu is equally impressive. Dishes like the Snake River Farms Wagyu burger, roasted root vegetable salad, and Idaho trout are all prepared with ingredients sourced from nearby farms and ranches.

- **Why It's Special**: Bittercreek's commitment to sustainability extends beyond its food. The restaurant is also involved in initiatives like composting, recycling, and energy conservation, making it a leader in Boise's green dining movement.

c. Fork

- **Overview**: Located in the heart of downtown Boise, Fork is a popular spot that prides itself on serving "loyal to local" cuisine. The restaurant sources the majority of its ingredients from Idaho and the Pacific Northwest, ensuring that every dish is fresh, flavorful, and reflective of the region's bounty.

- **Menu Highlights**: Fork's menu offers a mix of comfort food and contemporary dishes, with standouts like the Idaho rainbow trout, wild mushroom risotto, and "Farmers Market" salad, which features a rotating selection of fresh, seasonal vegetables. The restaurant also offers a variety of craft cocktails, wines, and beers, many of which are locally produced.

- **Why It's Special**: Fork's warm, inviting atmosphere and commitment to local sourcing make it a must-visit for anyone interested in experiencing Boise's farm-to-table dining. The restaurant's dedication to quality and sustainability is evident in every bite.

d. Wild Root Café & Market

- **Overview**: Wild Root Café & Market is a downtown Boise gem that focuses on health-conscious, farm-to-table cuisine. The café's menu is full of vibrant, fresh dishes that cater to a variety of dietary preferences, including vegan, vegetarian, and gluten-free options.

- **Menu Highlights**: Popular dishes at Wild Root include the avocado toast with local microgreens, the seasonal vegetable bowl with quinoa and tahini sauce, and the house-made granola with fresh fruit. The café also offers freshly pressed juices, smoothies, and a selection of locally sourced coffee and teas.

- **Why It's Special**: Wild Root's commitment to using organic, non-GMO ingredients, and its focus on wellness make it a favorite for those looking for healthy, delicious meals. The café's bright, airy atmosphere and friendly service add to the overall experience.

e. Red Feather Lounge

- **Overview**: Adjacent to Bittercreek Alehouse, Red Feather Lounge offers a more upscale farm-to-table dining experience. The restaurant's menu is inspired by seasonal ingredients and features a blend of classic and contemporary dishes, all prepared with the finest local produce and meats.

- **Menu Highlights**: Dishes like the roasted beet salad, lamb shank with local root vegetables, and the house-cured charcuterie board showcase the restaurant's dedication to quality and creativity. Red Feather also boasts an impressive wine list and craft cocktail menu, with many ingredients sourced from local distilleries and wineries.

- **Why It's Special**: Red Feather Lounge combines a sophisticated atmosphere with a genuine commitment to farm-to-table dining. The restaurant's focus on local ingredients and artisanal preparation makes it a standout in Boise's culinary scene.

3. FARMERS MARKETS AND LOCAL PRODUCERS

In addition to dining out, Boise's farm-to-table movement is supported by a vibrant network of farmers markets and local producers. These markets provide residents and visitors with direct access to the freshest ingredients, from organic vegetables and fruits to artisanal cheeses, meats, and baked goods.

a. Boise Farmers Market

- **Overview**: The Boise Farmers Market is a year-round market that operates on Saturdays, offering a wide range of local produce, meats, cheeses, baked goods, and more. The market is a great place to meet local farmers, sample fresh products, and stock up on seasonal ingredients.

- **Why It's Special**: The market emphasizes sustainable farming practices and supports small-scale, local producers. It's a hub of the community, where you can find everything from fresh vegetables and fruits to handmade crafts and ready-to-eat meals.

b. Capital City Public Market

- **Overview**: Another popular market in downtown Boise, the Capital City Public Market operates from April through December and features a diverse array of vendors selling fresh produce, flowers, prepared foods, and local crafts.

- **Why It's Special**: The market is a bustling, lively place that brings together the best of Boise's local food scene. It's a great spot to pick up ingredients for a farm-to-table meal at home or to enjoy a snack while exploring the city.

c. Local Farms and Artisans

- **Peaceful Belly Farm**: Located just outside Boise, Peaceful Belly Farm is a certified organic farm that supplies many of the city's restaurants with fresh produce. The farm also offers a CSA (Community Supported Agriculture) program, allowing locals to purchase shares of the harvest.

- **Highland Hollow Brewhouse**: This local brewery not only produces craft beers but also raises its own livestock, supplying pork and beef to several Boise restaurants. Their commitment to sustainable, ethical farming practices is reflected in the quality of their products.

4. WHY FARM-TO-TABLE MATTERS

The farm-to-table movement in Boise is about more than just great food—it's about fostering a connection between the land, the people who grow our food, and the community that enjoys it. By supporting farm-to-table dining, you're not only treating yourself to fresh, delicious meals but also contributing to a sustainable, local food system that benefits everyone.

a. Environmental Benefits

- **Reduced Carbon Footprint**: By sourcing ingredients locally, farm-to-table restaurants reduce the need for long-distance transportation, which in turn lowers the carbon footprint associated with food production and distribution.

- **Support for Sustainable Agriculture**: Farm-to-table dining encourages sustainable farming practices that prioritize soil health, biodiversity, and responsible water use. This helps protect the environment for future generations.

b. Community Impact

- **Supporting Local Economies**: Farm-to-table restaurants help keep money within the local economy by supporting farmers, ranchers, and food artisans in the area. This creates jobs and strengthens the community.

- **Building Connections**: The farm-to-table movement fosters connections between diners and the people who grow their food, creating a sense of community and shared purpose. This connection enriches the dining experience and encourages a greater appreciation for the food we eat.

7.2 TOP RESTAURANTS: FROM CASUAL EATS TO FINE DINING

Whether you're in the mood for a casual bite or a sophisticated dining experience, Boise has something to offer. Here's a guide to some of the top restaurants in the city, from laid-back spots perfect for a quick meal to fine dining establishments for special occasions.

1. CASUAL EATS

a. Big City Coffee & Café

- **Overview**: Big City Coffee & Café is a beloved Boise institution known for its hearty breakfasts, homemade pastries, and strong coffee. The café has a warm, welcoming atmosphere, making it a favorite spot for locals to gather.

- **Menu Highlights**: The café offers a wide range of breakfast and lunch options, including their famous oversized cinnamon rolls, breakfast burritos, and fresh salads. Their coffee menu features locally roasted beans, ensuring a perfect cup every time.

- **Address**: 1416 W Grove St, Boise, ID 83702

b. Boise Fry Company

- **Overview**: Boise Fry Company is a must-visit for anyone looking to try Idaho's famous potatoes in a variety of forms. The restaurant specializes in gourmet fries and burgers, with a focus on quality ingredients and sustainable practices.

- **Menu Highlights**: Choose from a variety of potato types and cuts, then pair your fries with one of their delicious burgers made from local, grass-fed beef. Don't forget to try their house-made dipping sauces for the full experience.

- **Address**: 204 N Capitol Blvd, Boise, ID 83702

c. Westside Drive-In

- **Overview**: Westside Drive-In is a retro-style diner offering classic American comfort food with a touch of nostalgia. Known for its friendly service and quirky menu items, it's a great spot for a fun, casual meal.

- **Menu Highlights**: Signature dishes include the Prime Rib Dinner, Idaho Ice Cream Potato (a dessert), and a variety of burgers, fries, and milkshakes. It's the perfect place to enjoy a taste of classic Americana.

- **Address**: 1939 W State St, Boise, ID 83702

d. The Modern Hotel and Bar

- **Overview**: The Modern Hotel and Bar is a trendy spot known for its farm-to-table menu and chic atmosphere. Located in the Linen District, it's a great place to enjoy a casual yet stylish meal.

- **Menu Highlights**: The menu features seasonal, locally sourced dishes like smoked trout salad, local beef tartare, and house-made pastas. The bar offers craft cocktails made with local spirits and fresh ingredients.

- **Address**: 1314 W Grove St, Boise, ID 83702

2. MID-RANGE DINING

a. Fork

- **Overview**: Fork is a popular downtown Boise restaurant that emphasizes "loyal to local" cuisine, with a menu that highlights the best of Idaho and the Pacific Northwest. The atmosphere is cozy and inviting, perfect for a relaxed meal with family or friends.

- **Menu Highlights**: Dishes like Idaho rainbow trout, wild mushroom risotto, and the "Farmers Market" salad showcase the region's bounty. Fork also offers a great selection of local wines, beers, and craft cocktails.

- **Address**: 199 N 8th St, Boise, ID 83702

b. Bittercreek Alehouse

- **Overview**: Bittercreek Alehouse is a downtown favorite known for its extensive selection of local beers and its commitment to sustainable, farm-to-table dining. The atmosphere is lively and casual, making it a great spot for any occasion.

- **Menu Highlights**: Popular dishes include the Snake River Farms Wagyu burger, roasted root vegetable salad, and Idaho trout. The rotating beer menu features a wide variety of local brews, ensuring there's always something new to try.

- **Address**: 246 N 8th St, Boise, ID 83702

c. Wild Root Café & Market

- **Overview**: Wild Root Café & Market is a downtown Boise spot that focuses on health-conscious, farm-to-table cuisine. The café's bright, airy atmosphere and fresh, vibrant dishes make it a popular choice for breakfast, lunch, and brunch.

- **Menu Highlights**: The menu includes options like avocado toast with local microgreens, seasonal vegetable bowls with quinoa, and house-made granola with fresh fruit. Wild Root also offers a selection of freshly pressed juices and smoothies.

- **Address**: 276 N 8th St, Boise, ID 83702

d. The Matador

- **Overview**: The Matador is a family-friendly Mexican restaurant known for its vibrant décor and flavorful dishes. It's a great spot for casual dining with a festive atmosphere.

- **Menu Highlights**: The menu features a variety of Mexican favorites, including tacos, enchiladas, and burritos. The Matador is also known for its extensive tequila selection and creative margaritas.

- **Address**: 215 N 8th St, Boise, ID 83702

3. FINE DINING

a. Chandler's

- **Overview**: Chandler's is a premier steakhouse and seafood restaurant in Boise, known for its elegant atmosphere, live jazz music, and impeccable service. It's the perfect place for a special night out or a celebration.

- **Menu Highlights**: Chandler's offers a selection of premium steaks, fresh seafood, and classic American dishes. Signature items include the Filet Mignon, Lobster Tail, and their famous 10-Minute Martini. The extensive wine list complements the menu perfectly.

- **Address**: 981 W Grove St, Boise, ID 83702

b. Capitol Cellars

- **Overview**: Capitol Cellars is an upscale restaurant and wine bar located in the historic Belgravia building in downtown Boise. The restaurant offers a refined dining experience with a focus on locally sourced ingredients and an impressive wine selection.

- **Menu Highlights**: The menu features dishes like Idaho trout, prime rib, and house-made pastas, all expertly paired with wines from their extensive cellar. Capitol Cellars is also known for its beautiful, intimate setting, perfect for a romantic dinner or special occasion.

- **Address**: 110 S 5th St, Boise, ID 83702

c. Richard's Restaurant & Bar

- **Overview**: Located in the Inn at 500 Capitol, Richard's Restaurant & Bar offers contemporary American cuisine with Mediterranean influences. The restaurant's elegant setting and creative menu make it a top choice for fine dining in Boise.

- **Menu Highlights**: Dishes like the pan-seared scallops, duck breast with cherry compote, and house-made pasta showcase the chef's skill and dedication to using the finest ingredients. The wine list and cocktail menu are equally impressive, featuring selections from around the world.

- **Address**: 500 S Capitol Blvd, Boise, ID 83702

d. Àlavita

- **Overview**: Àlavita is a fine dining Italian restaurant in downtown Boise, known for its focus on handmade pasta and fresh, seasonal ingredients. The restaurant's warm, inviting atmosphere and attentive service make it a favorite for special occasions.

- **Menu Highlights**: The menu features dishes like pappardelle with wild boar ragu, ricotta gnocchi with sage brown butter, and seared scallops with polenta. Àlavita also offers a carefully curated selection of Italian wines and house-made desserts.

- **Address**: 807 W Idaho St, Boise, ID 83702

7.3 BOISE'S CRAFT BEER SCENE: BREWERIES AND TAPROOMS

Boise boasts a vibrant culinary scene, offering a wide range of dining options to suit every palate and occasion. Whether you're in the mood for a casual bite or a sophisticated dining experience, Boise has something to offer. Here's a guide to some of the top restaurants in the city, from laid-back spots perfect for a quick meal to fine dining establishments for special occasions.

1. CASUAL EATS

a. Big City Coffee & Café

- **Overview**: Big City Coffee & Café is a beloved Boise institution known for its hearty breakfasts, homemade pastries, and strong coffee. The café has a warm, welcoming atmosphere, making it a favorite spot for locals to gather.

- **Menu Highlights**: The café offers a wide range of breakfast and lunch options, including their famous oversized cinnamon rolls, breakfast burritos, and fresh salads. Their coffee menu features locally roasted beans, ensuring a perfect cup every time.

- **Address**: 1416 W Grove St, Boise, ID 83702

b. Boise Fry Company

- **Overview**: Boise Fry Company is a must-visit for anyone looking to try Idaho's famous potatoes in a variety of forms. The restaurant specializes in gourmet fries and burgers, with a focus on quality ingredients and sustainable practices.

- **Menu Highlights**: Choose from a variety of potato types and cuts, then pair your fries with one of their delicious burgers made from local, grass-fed beef. Don't forget to try their house-made dipping sauces for the full experience.

- **Address**: 204 N Capitol Blvd, Boise, ID 83702

c. Westside Drive-In

- **Overview**: Westside Drive-In is a retro-style diner offering classic American comfort food with a touch of nostalgia. Known for its friendly service and quirky menu items, it's a great spot for a fun, casual meal.

- **Menu Highlights**: Signature dishes include the Prime Rib Dinner, Idaho Ice Cream Potato (a dessert), and a variety of burgers, fries, and milkshakes. It's the perfect place to enjoy a taste of classic Americana.

- **Address**: 1939 W State St, Boise, ID 83702

d. The Modern Hotel and Bar

- **Overview**: The Modern Hotel and Bar is a trendy spot known for its farm-to-table menu and chic atmosphere. Located in the Linen District, it's a great place to enjoy a casual yet stylish meal.

- **Menu Highlights**: The menu features seasonal, locally sourced dishes like smoked trout salad, local beef tartare, and house-made pastas. The bar offers craft cocktails made with local spirits and fresh ingredients.

- **Address**: 1314 W Grove St, Boise, ID 83702

2. MID-RANGE DINING

a. Fork

- **Overview**: Fork is a popular downtown Boise restaurant that emphasizes "loyal to local" cuisine, with a menu that highlights the best of Idaho and the Pacific Northwest. The atmosphere is cozy and inviting, perfect for a relaxed meal with family or friends.

- **Menu Highlights**: Dishes like Idaho rainbow trout, wild mushroom risotto, and the "Farmers Market" salad showcase the region's bounty. Fork also offers a great selection of local wines, beers, and craft cocktails.

- **Address**: 199 N 8th St, Boise, ID 83702

b. Bittercreek Alehouse

- **Overview**: Bittercreek Alehouse is a downtown favorite known for its extensive selection of local beers and its commitment to sustainable, farm-to-table dining. The atmosphere is lively and casual, making it a great spot for any occasion.

- **Menu Highlights**: Popular dishes include the Snake River Farms Wagyu burger, roasted root vegetable salad, and Idaho trout. The rotating beer menu features a wide variety of local brews, ensuring there's always something new to try.

- **Address**: 246 N 8th St, Boise, ID 83702

c. Wild Root Café & Market

- **Overview**: Wild Root Café & Market is a downtown Boise spot that focuses on health-conscious, farm-to-table cuisine. The café's bright, airy atmosphere and fresh, vibrant dishes make it a popular choice for breakfast, lunch, and brunch.

- **Menu Highlights**: The menu includes options like avocado toast with local microgreens, seasonal vegetable bowls with quinoa, and house-made granola with fresh fruit. Wild Root also offers a selection of freshly pressed juices and smoothies.

- **Address**: 276 N 8th St, Boise, ID 83702

d. The Matador

- **Overview**: The Matador is a family-friendly Mexican restaurant known for its vibrant décor and flavorful dishes. It's a great spot for casual dining with a festive atmosphere.

- **Menu Highlights**: The menu features a variety of Mexican favorites, including tacos, enchiladas, and burritos. The Matador is also known for its extensive tequila selection and creative margaritas.

- **Address**: 215 N 8th St, Boise, ID 83702

3. FINE DINING

a. Chandler's

- **Overview**: Chandler's is a premier steakhouse and seafood restaurant in Boise, known for its elegant atmosphere, live jazz music, and impeccable service. It's the perfect place for a special night out or a celebration.

- **Menu Highlights**: Chandler's offers a selection of premium steaks, fresh seafood, and classic American dishes. Signature items include the Filet Mignon, Lobster Tail, and their famous 10-Minute Martini. The extensive wine list complements the menu perfectly.

- **Address**: 981 W Grove St, Boise, ID 83702

b. Capitol Cellars

- **Overview**: Capitol Cellars is an upscale restaurant and wine bar located in the historic Belgravia building in downtown Boise. The restaurant offers a refined dining experience with a focus on locally sourced ingredients and an impressive wine selection.

- **Menu Highlights**: The menu features dishes like Idaho trout, prime rib, and house-made pastas, all expertly paired with wines from their extensive cellar. Capitol Cellars is also known for its beautiful, intimate setting, perfect for a romantic dinner or special occasion.

- **Address**: 110 S 5th St, Boise, ID 83702

c. Richard's Restaurant & Bar

- **Overview**: Located in the Inn at 500 Capitol, Richard's Restaurant & Bar offers contemporary American cuisine with Mediterranean influences. The restaurant's elegant setting and creative menu make it a top choice for fine dining in Boise.

- **Menu Highlights**: Dishes like the pan-seared scallops, duck breast with cherry compote, and house-made pasta showcase the chef's skill and dedication to using the finest ingredients. The wine list and cocktail menu are equally impressive, featuring selections from around the world.

- **Address**: 500 S Capitol Blvd, Boise, ID 83702

d. Àlavita

- **Overview**: Àlavita is a fine dining Italian restaurant in downtown Boise, known for its focus on handmade pasta and fresh, seasonal ingredients. The restaurant's warm, inviting atmosphere and attentive service make it a favorite for special occasions.

- **Menu Highlights**: The menu features dishes like pappardelle with wild boar ragu, ricotta gnocchi with sage brown butter, and seared scallops with polenta. Àlavita also offers a carefully curated selection of Italian wines and house-made desserts.

- **Address**: 807 W Idaho St, Boise, ID 83702

4. CONCLUSION

Boise's diverse culinary scene offers something for everyone, whether you're looking for a quick bite at a casual eatery or a memorable meal at one of the city's fine dining establishments. With a strong emphasis on local ingredients and innovative cooking, Boise's restaurants provide a taste of the region's best flavors and hospitality. Whether you're a resident or a visitor, these top dining spots are sure to impress and satisfy your cravings.

BOISE'S CRAFT BEER SCENE: BREWERIES AND TAPROOMS

Boise has quickly become a hotspot for craft beer enthusiasts, with a thriving scene that includes a wide array of breweries and taprooms offering unique, locally brewed beers. Whether you're a fan of hoppy IPAs, rich stouts, or crisp lagers, Boise's craft beer scene has something to satisfy every palate. Here's a guide to some of the top breweries and taprooms in Boise where you can enjoy fresh, locally crafted beers.

1. PAYETTE BREWING COMPANY

- **Overview**: Payette Brewing Company is one of Boise's largest and most popular breweries. Founded in 2010, Payette has become a staple of the local craft beer scene, known for its innovative brews and community-focused events. The brewery's spacious taproom and outdoor beer garden make it a great spot to relax with friends and enjoy a pint.

- **Signature Beers**: Payette Brewing offers a wide range of beers, with something for every taste. Popular choices include the Rustler IPA, North Fork Lager, and Rodeo Citra Pale Ale. Seasonal and limited-edition brews are also frequently available.

- **Address**: 733 S Pioneer St, Boise, ID 83702

- **Why It's Special**: Payette's taproom features a laid-back atmosphere with games, food trucks, and frequent live music. The brewery is also dog-friendly, making it a perfect spot to bring your furry friends.

2. SOCKEYE BREWING

- **Overview**: Sockeye Brewing is a veteran of the Boise craft beer scene, having brewed its first batch of beer in 1996. The brewery is known for its commitment to quality and its focus on using the best local ingredients. Sockeye operates two locations in Boise: the original brewpub and a larger production facility with a taproom.

- **Signature Beers**: Sockeye's beers are consistently well-crafted, with popular offerings like the Dagger Falls IPA, Angel's Perch Amber Ale, and Powerhouse Porter. The brewery also produces a variety of seasonal and specialty beers throughout the year.

- **Address**:

  - Brewpub: 3019 N Cole Rd, Boise, ID 83704

  - Taproom & Brewery: 12542 W Fairview Ave, Boise, ID 83713

- **Why It's Special**: Sockeye Brewing's locations offer a cozy, welcoming atmosphere with great food and a rotating selection of fresh beers on tap. The brewpub is a favorite for its hearty pub fare, while the taproom provides a more industrial, beer-focused experience.

3. BOISE BREWING

- **Overview**: Boise Brewing is a community-supported brewery located in the heart of downtown Boise. The brewery was founded with the help of local investors and has quickly become a beloved part of the city's craft beer community. Boise Brewing is known for its diverse lineup of beers and its active involvement in local events and causes.

- **Signature Beers**: Popular beers from Boise Brewing include the Snowboarder Porter, Broad Street Blonde, and Hip Check IPA. The brewery frequently experiments with new styles and flavors, offering a rotating selection of seasonal and limited-edition brews.

- **Address**: 521 W Broad St, Boise, ID 83702

- **Why It's Special**: Boise Brewing's taproom is a vibrant, lively space where you can enjoy a beer while chatting with friends or participating in one of the brewery's many events, such as trivia nights or beer release parties. The brewery's community-oriented approach makes it a welcoming spot for locals and visitors alike.

4. BARBARIAN BREWING

- **Overview**: Barbarian Brewing is a small, independent brewery with a focus on barrel-aged and sour beers. Founded in 2015, Barbarian has quickly made a name for itself with its creative and complex brews that push the boundaries of traditional beer styles. The brewery operates two locations: the main brewery in Garden City and a downtown Boise taproom.

- **Signature Beers**: Barbarian is known for its innovative sour and barrel-aged beers, such as the Sanguis Mortuum Blood Orange Sour and the Viking's Lament Bourbon Barrel-Aged Stout. The brewery also offers a variety of IPAs, lagers, and other styles for those looking for something different.

- **Address**:

  o   Brewery & Taproom: 114 E 32nd St, Garden City, ID 83714

  o   Downtown Taproom: 1022 W Main St, Boise, ID 83702

- **Why It's Special**: Barbarian Brewing's taprooms offer a unique experience for beer lovers looking to try something new and different. The intimate, cozy atmosphere and knowledgeable staff make it a great place to explore the more adventurous side of craft beer.

5. LOST GROVE BREWING

- **Overview**: Lost Grove Brewing is a newer addition to Boise's craft beer scene, having opened its doors in 2017. The brewery is committed to sustainability and community involvement, with a focus on producing high-quality, environmentally friendly beers. Lost Grove's taproom is a welcoming space with a laid-back vibe.

- **Signature Beers**: Lost Grove's flagship beers include the Teddy Bear Picnic Golden Ale, River Party Pale Ale, and Highlands Hollow Hazy IPA. The brewery also produces a range of seasonal and specialty beers that showcase local ingredients and creative brewing techniques.

- **Address**: 1026 S La Pointe St, Boise, ID 83706

- **Why It's Special**: Lost Grove's commitment to sustainability is evident in everything they do, from their brewing process to their community initiatives. The taproom's relaxed atmosphere, combined with the brewery's dedication to quality and innovation, makes it a must-visit spot for craft beer enthusiasts.

6. WOODLAND EMPIRE ALE CRAFT

- **Overview**: Woodland Empire Ale Craft is known for its experimental approach to brewing, offering a wide range of unique and flavorful beers. The brewery has a reputation for pushing the boundaries of traditional beer styles, often incorporating unusual ingredients and techniques into their brews.

- **Signature Beers**: Woodland Empire's lineup includes a mix of core beers and rotating specialties. Popular options include the Big Sticky American IPA, Electric Warrior Stout, and the City of Trees IPA. The brewery also offers a variety of barrel-aged and sour beers for those looking for something different.

- **Address**: 1114 W Front St, Boise, ID 83702

- **Why It's Special**: Woodland Empire's taproom is a funky, eclectic space that reflects the brewery's creative spirit. The ever-changing beer menu means there's always something new to try, making it a favorite among adventurous beer drinkers.

7. CLOUD 9 BREWERY

- **Overview**: Cloud 9 Brewery is a small, family-owned brewery with a focus on organic, sustainable brewing practices. The brewery prides itself on using locally sourced, organic ingredients in all of its beers, resulting in fresh, clean flavors that reflect the best of Idaho's agricultural bounty.

- **Signature Beers**: Cloud 9's core beers include the Bavarian Hefeweizen, Belgian White, and Porter. The brewery also offers a rotating selection of seasonal and specialty beers, including barrel-aged varieties and experimental brews.

- **Address**: 1750 W State St, Boise, ID 83702

- **Why It's Special**: Cloud 9's commitment to sustainability and quality shines through in every aspect of their operation, from their organic ingredients to their eco-friendly brewing process. The taproom's cozy, welcoming atmosphere makes it a great place to enjoy a pint and relax with friends.

8. MOTHER EARTH BREW CO.

- **Overview**: Mother Earth Brew Co. is a California-based brewery that expanded to Idaho with a production facility and taproom in Nampa, just outside Boise. The brewery is known for its well-crafted, approachable beers that appeal to a wide range of tastes.

- **Signature Beers**: Popular beers from Mother Earth include the Cali Creamin' Vanilla Cream Ale, Boo Koo Mosaic IPA, and Sin Tax Imperial Stout. The brewery also offers a variety of seasonal and limited-edition beers, ensuring there's always something new to try.

- **Address**: 1428 Madison Ave, Nampa, ID 83687

- **Why It's Special**: Mother Earth's Nampa facility offers a spacious taproom and beer garden where visitors can enjoy fresh beer straight from the source. The brewery's commitment to quality and consistency makes it a favorite among both locals and visitors.

9. MAD SWEDE BREWING COMPANY

- **Overview**: Mad Swede Brewing Company is a family-owned brewery with a focus on producing high-quality, handcrafted beers inspired by Scandinavian heritage. The brewery's taproom offers a welcoming atmosphere where you can enjoy a pint and learn more about the brewing process.

- **Signature Beers**: Mad Swede's lineup includes the Naked Sunbather Blonde Ale, Longship IPA, and Helm of Awe Porter. The brewery also offers a variety of seasonal and specialty brews, often with a nod to Nordic traditions.

- **Address**: 2772 S Cole Rd Ste 140, Boise, ID 83709

- **Why It's Special**: Mad Swede's unique approach to brewing, combined with its friendly, knowledgeable staff, makes it a standout in Boise's craft beer scene. The taproom's laid-back vibe and Scandinavian-inspired decor add to the overall experience.

10. EDGE BREWING COMPANY

- **Overview**: Edge Brewing Company is a well-established Boise brewery known for its wide range of craft beers and its lively brewpub atmosphere. The brewery offers a full menu of food options, making it a great spot for a meal as well as a pint.

- **Signature Beers**: Edge Brewing's popular beers include the Obligatory Pale Ale, Hop Kissed IPA, and Odelay Mexican Lager. The brewery also produces a variety of seasonal and specialty beers, often experimenting with different styles and flavors.

- **Address**: 525 N Steelhead Way, Boise, ID 83704

- **Why It's Special**: Edge Brewing's brewpub offers a fun, energetic atmosphere with a focus on great beer and delicious food. The brewery's commitment to innovation and quality ensures that there's always something new and exciting to try.

7.4 FARMERS MARKETS: FRESH PRODUCE AND LOCAL CRAFTS

Boise's farmers markets are vibrant community hubs where locals and visitors alike can find fresh produce, handmade crafts, artisanal foods, and more. These markets not only support local farmers and artisans but also offer a unique shopping experience that celebrates the best of Idaho's agricultural bounty and creative spirit. Here's a guide to some of the top farmers markets in Boise, where you can enjoy fresh, local products and discover one-of-a-kind crafts.

1. THE BOISE FARMERS MARKET

- **Overview**: The Boise Farmers Market is one of the city's premier markets, offering a wide variety of locally grown produce, artisanal foods, and handmade crafts. It's a must-visit for anyone looking to experience the best of Idaho's agriculture and culinary creativity.

- **What to Expect**: The market features dozens of vendors selling everything from fresh vegetables, fruits, and herbs to baked goods, cheeses, meats, and more. You'll also find food trucks, live music, and community events that make the market a lively and enjoyable place to spend your Saturday morning.

- **Local Crafts**: In addition to fresh produce, the market showcases a selection of locally made crafts, including handmade jewelry, pottery, textiles, and woodworking. These crafts make great souvenirs or gifts and highlight the talent of Idaho's artisans.

- **Location and Hours**: The Boise Farmers Market is held every Saturday from April through December at 1500 Shoreline Dr, Boise, ID 83702, from 9:00 AM to 1:00 PM.

- **Why It's Special**: The Boise Farmers Market emphasizes sustainable farming practices and supports local producers, making it a great place to shop with confidence. The market's commitment to fresh, local products and its community-focused atmosphere make it a beloved part of Boise's food scene.

2. CAPITAL CITY PUBLIC MARKET

- **Overview**: The Capital City Public Market is another popular farmers market in downtown Boise, known for its diverse selection of vendors and its central location. Established in 1994, this market has become a Saturday tradition for many Boise residents.

- **What to Expect**: The market offers a wide range of products, including fresh produce, meats, cheeses, baked goods, and prepared foods. In addition to food items, the market features a variety of local crafts, including clothing, artwork, and home décor.

- **Local Crafts**: The Capital City Public Market is a great place to find unique, handmade items from local artisans. Whether you're looking for a piece of art, a handcrafted candle, or a custom piece of jewelry, you're sure to find something special.

- **Location and Hours**: The market takes place on 8th Street in downtown Boise from April through December, every Saturday from 9:30 AM to 1:30 PM.

- **Why It's Special**: The Capital City Public Market is more than just a place to shop—it's a social event that brings the community together. With its lively atmosphere, variety of vendors, and downtown location, the market is a great way to start your weekend and connect with the Boise community.

3. NAMPA FARMERS MARKET

- **Overview**: Located just a short drive from Boise, the Nampa Farmers Market is a charming, family-friendly market that offers a wide selection of fresh produce, local crafts, and live entertainment. It's a great option for those looking to explore the broader Treasure Valley area.

- **What to Expect**: The Nampa Farmers Market features vendors selling everything from seasonal fruits and vegetables to homemade jams, honey, and baked goods. The market also offers a variety of locally made crafts, including woodworking, textiles, and handcrafted jewelry.

- **Local Crafts**: The market's selection of crafts is diverse, with many items reflecting the unique character and creativity of the local artisans. You'll find everything from rustic home décor to finely crafted leather goods.

- **Location and Hours**: The Nampa Farmers Market is held every Saturday from April through October at Lloyd Square Park in downtown Nampa, from 9:00 AM to 1:00 PM.

- **Why It's Special**: The Nampa Farmers Market offers a relaxed, small-town atmosphere with a strong sense of community. The market's mix of fresh produce, local crafts, and live entertainment makes it a fun and engaging destination for the whole family.

4. EAGLE SATURDAY MARKET

- **Overview**: The Eagle Saturday Market, located in the nearby town of Eagle, is a quaint and charming market that offers a mix of fresh produce, handmade crafts, and live music. It's a great spot for a leisurely Saturday morning outing.

- **What to Expect**: The market features a variety of vendors selling fresh fruits, vegetables, herbs, and flowers, as well as a selection of locally made foods and crafts. The market's laid-back vibe and scenic location make it a favorite among locals and visitors alike.

- **Local Crafts**: The Eagle Saturday Market showcases a range of handcrafted items, including jewelry, pottery, clothing, and artwork. These unique, locally made products reflect the creativity and craftsmanship of the Eagle community.

- **Location and Hours**: The market takes place in Heritage Park, Eagle, every Saturday from May through October, from 9:00 AM to 1:00 PM.

- **Why It's Special**: The Eagle Saturday Market is known for its friendly, welcoming atmosphere and its focus on community. The market's smaller size and relaxed pace make it a great place to browse, shop, and enjoy a quiet morning in a beautiful setting.

5. EMMETT FARMERS MARKET

- **Overview**: The Emmett Farmers Market, located about 30 miles northwest of Boise, is a small, community-oriented market that offers fresh produce, local crafts, and a taste of rural Idaho. It's a great destination for those looking to explore beyond Boise.

- **What to Expect**: The market features a variety of vendors selling locally grown fruits and vegetables, homemade baked goods, and other farm-fresh products. You'll also find a selection of handcrafted items, including woodworking, textiles, and home décor.

- **Local Crafts**: The Emmett Farmers Market is a great place to find unique, handcrafted items that reflect the rural charm and creativity of the local artisans. Whether you're looking for a handmade quilt, a piece of pottery, or a custom piece of jewelry, you'll find plenty of options here.

- **Location and Hours**: The market is held every Saturday from June through September at Blaser Park, Emmett, from 8:00 AM to 12:00 PM.

- **Why It's Special**: The Emmett Farmers Market offers a glimpse into the agricultural heart of Idaho, with fresh produce and crafts that reflect the traditions and values of the local community. The market's small size and friendly atmosphere make it a pleasant and rewarding place to visit.

Chapter 8: Cultural Experiences and Local Traditions

8.1 Basque Block: A Taste of Boise's Unique Heritage

The Basque Block in Boise is a vibrant testament to the city's rich cultural tapestry, offering visitors a unique opportunity to experience the heritage, traditions, and flavors of the Basque people. Nestled in the heart of downtown Boise, this historic district is home to one of the largest Basque communities in the United States and serves as a lively hub for Basque culture in the region. Whether you're interested in history, cuisine, or simply soaking up the atmosphere, the Basque Block is a must-visit destination that provides a fascinating glimpse into Boise's diverse cultural landscape.

1. The History of Boise's Basque Community

Boise's Basque community traces its roots back to the late 19th and early 20th centuries when Basque immigrants began arriving in Idaho in search of new opportunities. Many of these immigrants came from the Basque Country, a region that straddles the border between Spain and France, and brought with them their unique language, customs, and traditions. Initially working as sheepherders, the Basque people quickly established a close-knit community in Boise, preserving their heritage while also contributing to the city's development.

- **Basque Sheepherders**: The Basque immigrants were primarily known for their work as sheepherders in the rugged mountains of Idaho. This occupation not only shaped their economic contribution but also influenced their cultural practices, many of which are still celebrated today.

- **Community and Preservation**: Over the years, the Basque community in Boise has grown and thrived, making significant efforts to preserve their language, culture, and traditions. The Basque Block stands as a symbol of these efforts, showcasing the community's pride in their heritage.

2. EXPLORING THE BASQUE BLOCK

The Basque Block, located on Grove Street between Capitol Boulevard and 6th Street, is the heart of Boise's Basque community. This pedestrian-friendly area is lined with historic buildings, cultural institutions, and eateries that offer a deep dive into Basque heritage. Here's what you can explore on the Basque Block:

a. The Basque Museum & Cultural Center

- **Overview**: The Basque Museum & Cultural Center is the cornerstone of the Basque Block, dedicated to preserving and sharing the history and culture of the Basque people in Idaho. It's the only Basque museum in the United States and offers a rich collection of exhibits and artifacts.

- **Exhibits and Highlights**: The museum features permanent and rotating exhibits on Basque history, traditional clothing, music, and the role of Basques in Idaho's sheepherding industry. Visitors can also explore the historic Cyrus Jacobs-Uberuaga House, the oldest brick building in Boise and a former boarding house for Basque immigrants.

- **Educational Programs**: The museum offers educational programs, language classes, and cultural workshops, making it a center for learning and cultural exchange. It's a great place to start your visit to the Basque Block and gain a deeper understanding of the community's history.

- **Address**: 611 W Grove St, Boise, ID 83702

b. The Basque Market

- **Overview**: The Basque Market is a charming, authentic market and café that offers a taste of Basque cuisine right in the heart of Boise. It's a popular spot for both locals and visitors looking to enjoy traditional Basque flavors in a casual, friendly setting.

- **Menu Highlights**: The Basque Market is known for its pintxos (Basque-style tapas), which are small, flavorful bites that can be enjoyed with a glass of wine or cider. Other popular menu items include paella, chorizo, and Basque cheese platters. The market also offers a selection of imported Basque products, including wines, cheeses, and specialty foods.

- **Paella on the Patio**: One of the market's most beloved traditions is the weekly "Paella on the Patio" event, where a giant pan of paella is cooked outdoors and served to guests. This lively, communal meal is a great way to experience Basque hospitality and enjoy a delicious, authentic dish.

- **Address**: 608 W Grove St, Boise, ID 83702

c. Bar Gernika

- **Overview**: Bar Gernika is a cozy Basque pub located on the Basque Block, offering a welcoming atmosphere and a menu filled with traditional Basque dishes. The bar is named after the town of Gernika in the Basque Country, which holds significant historical and cultural importance for the Basque people.

- **Menu Highlights**: Bar Gernika is famous for its lamb grinders, croquetas, and solomo sandwiches (pork loin with pimientos). The bar also serves a variety of Basque beers, ciders, and wines, making it a great spot to relax and enjoy a meal or drink with friends.

- **Cultural Significance**: Bar Gernika has been a staple of the Basque Block for decades, serving as a gathering place for the local Basque community and visitors alike. Its warm, friendly atmosphere and authentic cuisine make it a must-visit destination on the Basque Block.

- **Address**: 202 S Capitol Blvd, Boise, ID 83702

d. Leku Ona

- **Overview**: Leku Ona, which means "Good Place" in Basque, is a fine dining restaurant that offers an upscale Basque dining experience. Located in a historic building on the Basque Block, Leku Ona provides a warm, elegant setting for enjoying traditional Basque dishes.

- **Menu Highlights**: The menu at Leku Ona features a variety of Basque specialties, including bacalao (salted cod), chuleta (grilled ribeye), and lamb shank. The restaurant also offers an extensive wine list featuring Basque and Spanish wines, making it a perfect spot for a special occasion or a leisurely dinner.

- **Authentic Atmosphere**: Leku Ona's commitment to authenticity extends beyond its menu. The restaurant's décor and ambiance reflect the rich cultural heritage of the Basque Country, providing diners with a truly immersive experience.

- **Address**: 117 S 6th St, Boise, ID 83702

e. Basque Festivals and Events

- **San Inazio Festival**: One of the most significant events on the Basque Block is the annual San Inazio Festival, held in late July. This festival celebrates St. Ignatius of Loyola, the patron saint of the Basque Country, with a weekend of music, dance, food, and traditional Basque sports. The festival attracts visitors from all over the region and is a vibrant showcase of Basque culture.

- **Sheepherders Ball**: Another popular event is the Sheepherders Ball, held every December. This festive gathering includes live music, traditional Basque dancing, and a dinner featuring Basque cuisine. The ball is a celebration of the Basque sheepherding heritage and a cherished tradition for the local community.

- **Ongoing Events**: Throughout the year, the Basque Block hosts a variety of cultural events, including Basque language classes, cooking demonstrations, and musical performances. These events provide ongoing opportunities to engage with Basque culture and learn more about this unique community.

3. CULTURAL SIGNIFICANCE OF THE BASQUE BLOCK

The Basque Block is more than just a collection of buildings and businesses—it's a living representation of Boise's diverse cultural heritage and a testament to the resilience and contributions of the Basque people. The block serves as a focal point for preserving Basque traditions, language, and customs while also sharing them with the broader community.

- **Preservation of Heritage**: The Basque Block plays a crucial role in preserving the cultural heritage of the Basque community in Boise. Through its museums, restaurants, and events, the block keeps Basque traditions alive and ensures they are passed down to future generations.

- **Community and Identity**: For the Basque community in Boise, the Basque Block is a symbol of identity and pride. It provides a space for gathering, celebrating, and maintaining the cultural practices that have been an integral part of Boise's history for over a century.

- **Cultural Exchange**: The Basque Block also serves as a bridge between cultures, offering non-Basque visitors a chance to learn about and appreciate the rich traditions of the Basque people. It's a place where cultural exchange and understanding are fostered, contributing to the broader cultural fabric of Boise.

8.2 MUSIC AND ARTS FESTIVALS: YEAR-ROUND EVENTS

Whether you're into live music, visual arts, or theater, Boise has something to offer year-round. Here's a guide to some of the top music and arts festivals in Boise, each providing its own unique flavor and atmosphere.

1. TREEFORT MUSIC FEST

- **Overview**: Treefort Music Fest is Boise's premier music and arts festival, attracting thousands of visitors and artists from around the world. Launched in 2012, Treefort has quickly grown into one of the most anticipated events in the Pacific Northwest, offering a diverse lineup of music, film, art, and more.

- **When**: Late March

- **What to Expect**: Treefort spans five days and features hundreds of performances across various genres, including indie rock, hip-hop, electronic, and folk. In addition to music, the festival includes several "forts" dedicated to different arts and interests, such as Filmfort, Comedyfort, Foodfort, and Storyfort. It's a citywide celebration with events held in venues and outdoor spaces throughout downtown Boise.

- **Why It's Special**: Treefort is known for its eclectic lineup, inclusive atmosphere, and community-driven spirit. It's a festival that celebrates creativity in all forms, making it a must-attend event for music and arts lovers.

- **Location**: Various venues throughout downtown Boise

2. ART IN THE PARK

- **Overview**: Art in the Park is one of Boise's longest-running and most beloved arts festivals, organized by the Boise Art Museum. This outdoor festival transforms Julia Davis Park into a bustling marketplace of creativity, featuring artists and artisans from around the country.

- **When**: Early September

- **What to Expect**: The three-day event showcases a wide variety of art forms, including painting, sculpture, jewelry, ceramics, photography, and more. In addition to shopping for unique, handcrafted items, visitors can enjoy live music, food vendors, and interactive art activities for children.

- **Why It's Special**: Art in the Park is a cherished Boise tradition that brings together artists, collectors, and families in a beautiful outdoor setting. The festival offers a unique opportunity to purchase original art directly from the artists while supporting the Boise Art Museum.

- **Location**: Julia Davis Park, Boise, ID

3. BOISE MUSIC FESTIVAL

- **Overview**: The Boise Music Festival is one of the city's largest music events, attracting big-name performers as well as showcasing local talent. The festival offers a full day of music, entertainment, and family-friendly activities.

- **When**: Late June

- **What to Expect**: The Boise Music Festival features multiple stages with performances from national headliners, regional acts, and local musicians across a variety of genres. The festival also includes a carnival, food vendors, and a beer garden, making it a fun, all-ages event. Past headliners have included major artists from pop, rock, and country music.

- **Why It's Special**: The Boise Music Festival combines the excitement of a large-scale concert with the feel of a community event. It's a great way to kick off the summer and enjoy live music in a lively, outdoor setting.

- **Location**: Expo Idaho, 5610 N Glenwood St, Boise, ID 83714

4. FREAK ALLEY GALLERY MURAL FESTIVAL

- **Overview**: Freak Alley Gallery is one of Boise's most unique art spaces, known for its vibrant street art and murals. Each year, the gallery hosts a mural festival, where local and regional artists come together to create new works of public art in the alley.

- **When**: Early August

- **What to Expect**: The mural festival is a week-long event where artists transform the walls of Freak Alley into an ever-changing canvas of creativity. Visitors can watch the artists at work, engage with them about their process, and enjoy the finished pieces. The festival concludes with a block party, featuring live music, food trucks, and art vendors.

- **Why It's Special**: Freak Alley Gallery is one of the largest outdoor mural galleries in the Northwest, and the festival offers a rare opportunity to see artists in action. It's a celebration of street art and urban culture that adds color and creativity to Boise's downtown.

- **Location**: Freak Alley, 210 N 9th St, Boise, ID 83702

5. IDAHO SHAKESPEARE FESTIVAL

- **Overview**: The Idaho Shakespeare Festival is a beloved Boise tradition, offering professional theater productions in a stunning outdoor amphitheater. The festival has been a cornerstone of Boise's cultural scene for over four decades, attracting theatergoers of all ages.

- **When**: Late May through September

- **What to Expect**: The festival features a rotating lineup of Shakespearean classics, contemporary plays, and musicals performed by a talented cast of actors. The open-air amphitheater is located along the Boise River, providing a picturesque backdrop for an evening of theater under the stars. Audiences are encouraged to bring picnics, blankets, and lawn chairs for a relaxed, enjoyable experience.

- **Why It's Special**: The Idaho Shakespeare Festival combines world-class theater with the natural beauty of Boise's landscape. It's a cultural gem that offers both locals and visitors a chance to enjoy high-quality performances in a unique setting.

- **Location**: Idaho Shakespeare Festival Amphitheater, 5657 Warm Springs Ave, Boise, ID 83716

6. JAIALDI BASQUE FESTIVAL

- **Overview**: Jaialdi is one of the largest Basque festivals in the world, held every five years in Boise. This week-long event celebrates the rich cultural heritage of the Basque community with traditional music, dance, food, and sports.

- **When**: Late July (next scheduled for 2025)

- **What to Expect**: Jaialdi features a wide range of activities, including traditional Basque dancing, music performances, culinary events, and pelota (a Basque sport similar to handball). The festival also includes a large parade, cultural exhibitions, and a lively street fair on the Basque Block. Visitors can immerse themselves in Basque culture and enjoy the vibrant, communal atmosphere.

- **Why It's Special**: Jaialdi is a rare and extraordinary celebration of Basque culture, drawing participants and spectators from around the globe. It's an opportunity to experience a unique and vibrant cultural tradition that has deep roots in Boise.

- **Location**: Various locations throughout Boise, with a focus on the Basque Block

7. HYDE PARK STREET FAIR

- **Overview**: The Hyde Park Street Fair is a popular community event held in Boise's historic North End neighborhood. The fair offers a mix of live music, local crafts, food, and family-friendly activities in the picturesque setting of Camel's Back Park.

- **When**: Mid-September

- **What to Expect**: The Hyde Park Street Fair features multiple stages with performances by local bands, artisans selling handmade goods, a variety of food and drink vendors, and activities for children, including games and rides. The fair has a relaxed, neighborhood feel, making it a perfect way to spend a fall weekend.

- **Why It's Special**: The Hyde Park Street Fair is a true community event, reflecting the character and spirit of Boise's North End. It's a great place to enjoy live music, support local artisans, and connect with the Boise community.

- **Location**: Camel's Back Park, 1200 W Heron St, Boise, ID 83702

8. BOISE SOUL FOOD FESTIVAL

- **Overview**: The Boise Soul Food Festival is a celebration of African American culture, cuisine, and music, bringing the community together for a day of food, entertainment, and cultural exchange.

- **When**: Early August

- **What to Expect**: The festival features a variety of soul food vendors offering classic dishes like fried chicken, collard greens, mac and cheese, and sweet potato pie. In addition to the food, the festival includes live music performances, dance, and cultural exhibits. It's a lively, family-friendly event that highlights the contributions of African American culture to Boise.

- **Why It's Special**: The Boise Soul Food Festival is a unique and flavorful event that offers a taste of soul food and a celebration of

African American culture in the heart of Boise. It's a festival that brings people together to enjoy great food, music, and community.

- **Location**: Julia Davis Park, Boise, ID

9. BOISE CONTEMPORARY THEATER

- **Overview**: Boise Contemporary Theater (BCT) is the city's leading venue for contemporary theater, offering a season of innovative and thought-provoking plays. While not a festival in the traditional sense, BCT's programming is a key part of Boise's arts scene, with a focus on new works and contemporary voices.

- **When**: September through May (season schedule)

- **What to Expect**: BCT's season typically includes a mix of world premieres, regional premieres, and contemporary classics, with a focus on storytelling that reflects the diverse experiences and perspectives of today's world. The intimate theater setting allows for an engaging and immersive experience.

- **Why It's Special**: BCT is known for its bold programming and commitment to pushing the boundaries of contemporary theater. It's a cultural hub for Boise's arts community and a must-visit for anyone interested in cutting-edge performance art.

- **Location**: 854 Fulton St, Boise, ID 83702

8.3 BOISE CONTEMPORARY THEATER AND PERFORMING ARTS

Boise Contemporary Theater (BCT) is a cornerstone of Boise's thriving arts scene, dedicated to presenting bold, innovative, and thought-provoking theater. Since its founding in 1997, BCT has become the premier venue for contemporary theater in Idaho, offering audiences a unique blend of new works, regional premieres, and original productions that challenge, entertain, and inspire. Alongside BCT, Boise's performing arts community is rich with talent, offering a variety of performances throughout the year that cater to diverse artistic tastes.

1. Boise Contemporary Theater (BCT)

a. Mission and Vision

Mission: BCT's mission is to inspire, entertain, and provoke dialogue through the creation and presentation of bold and engaging theater. The theater is committed to producing contemporary works that reflect the complexities of modern life and resonate with today's audiences.

Vision: BCT envisions a community where theater is a vital part of cultural life, sparking conversation and connection among diverse audiences. The theater strives to be a hub for artistic innovation and a platform for new voices in the performing arts.

b. Programming and Productions

Seasonal Lineup: BCT's season typically runs from September through May and features a carefully curated lineup of plays that range from world premieres to contemporary classics. Each season includes a mix of genres, including drama, comedy, and experimental theater, ensuring there's something for everyone.

Original Works: One of BCT's hallmarks is its commitment to producing original works. The theater frequently collaborates with playwrights to develop and premiere new plays, giving audiences the opportunity to experience fresh, groundbreaking stories that often explore timely and relevant issues.

Regional Premieres: In addition to original productions, BCT is known for bringing regional premieres of acclaimed contemporary plays to Boise. These productions allow local audiences to experience cutting-edge theater that may not be available elsewhere in the region.

c. The Theater Experience

Intimate Setting: BCT's downtown Boise venue is designed to create an intimate and immersive theater experience. With seating for just over 200 people, the theater ensures that every seat is close to the action, allowing audiences to fully engage with the performances.

Community Engagement: BCT is deeply committed to engaging with the Boise community. The theater offers a variety of programs and events, including talkbacks with the cast and crew, workshops, and educational outreach initiatives. These opportunities allow audiences to gain deeper insights into the productions and the creative process.

Accessibility: BCT is dedicated to making theater accessible to all members of the community. The theater offers a range of ticket pricing options, including discounted tickets for students, seniors, and groups. BCT also provides accommodations for patrons with disabilities, ensuring that everyone can enjoy the performances.

d. Notable Productions

Recent Highlights: BCT has produced a number of standout productions in recent years, including original works like "Hand to God" by Robert Askins, "The Clean House" by Sarah Ruhl, and "A Nighttime Survival Guide" by Dwayne Blackaller and Matthew Cameron Clark. These productions have garnered critical acclaim and helped establish BCT as a leader in contemporary theater.

Community Favorites: BCT's programming often includes plays that resonate deeply with the Boise community, addressing themes such as identity, social justice, and human connection. The theater's ability to select works that speak to the local audience has made it a beloved institution in Boise's cultural landscape.

e. Location and Contact Information

Address: Boise Contemporary Theater is located at 854 Fulton St, Boise, ID 83702.

Contact: For more information about upcoming productions, ticketing, and special events, you can visit the BCT website or contact the box office at (208) 331-9224.

2. Performing Arts in Boise

Beyond Boise Contemporary Theater, the city is home to a vibrant performing arts community that includes theater, dance, music, and more. **Here are some of the key organizations and venues that contribute to Boise's rich cultural life:**

a. The Morrison Center for the Performing Arts

Overview: The Morrison Center is Boise's premier performing arts venue, located on the campus of Boise State University. With a seating capacity of over 2,000, the Morrison Center hosts a wide range of performances, including Broadway tours, concerts, ballet, opera, and more.

Programming: The Morrison Center's diverse lineup includes performances by national touring companies, as well as productions by local organizations such as Ballet Idaho, Opera Idaho, and the Boise Philharmonic. The venue is also home to the Broadway in Boise series, which brings popular Broadway shows to the city each year.

Address: 2201 W Cesar Chavez Ln, Boise, ID 83725

b. The Idaho Shakespeare Festival

Overview: The Idaho Shakespeare Festival is a beloved cultural institution that offers professional theater productions in a stunning outdoor amphitheater. The festival's season runs from late May through September and includes a mix of Shakespearean classics, contemporary plays, and musicals.

Unique Setting: The festival's amphitheater is located along the Boise River, providing a beautiful natural backdrop for evening performances. Audiences are encouraged to bring picnics and enjoy the relaxed, communal atmosphere.

Address: 5657 Warm Springs Ave, Boise, ID 83716

c. Ballet Idaho

Overview: Ballet Idaho is the state's premier professional ballet company, offering a full season of classical and contemporary ballet performances. The company is known for its high-quality productions and commitment to both tradition and innovation in dance.

Programming: Ballet Idaho's season typically includes beloved classics such as "The Nutcracker," as well as new works by contemporary choreographers. The company also offers educational programs and community outreach initiatives.

Performances: Most of Ballet Idaho's performances are held at the Morrison Center, providing audiences with a world-class theater experience.

Address: 501 S 8th St, Boise, ID 83702

d. Opera Idaho

Overview: Opera Idaho is dedicated to bringing the art of opera to the Boise community. The company presents a variety of productions each season, ranging from grand operas to chamber works and special concerts.

Programming: Opera Idaho's season includes full-scale productions of classic operas, as well as more intimate performances in smaller venues. The company also hosts educational events, including lectures, workshops, and opportunities for young artists.

Performances: Opera Idaho's mainstage productions are typically held at the Morrison Center, with additional performances and events at various venues throughout Boise.

Address: 513 S 8th St, Boise, ID 83702

e. The Boise Philharmonic

Overview: The Boise Philharmonic is the city's premier symphony orchestra, offering a full season of concerts that range from classical masterworks to pops performances. The Philharmonic is a cornerstone of Boise's music scene and plays a vital role in the cultural life of the community.

Programming: The Philharmonic's season includes a variety of concert series, including the Masterworks series, which features classical symphonies and concertos, and the Pops series, which showcases lighter, more popular repertoire. The orchestra also collaborates with Ballet Idaho and Opera Idaho for special performances.

Performances: Most Boise Philharmonic concerts are held at the Morrison Center, with additional performances at other venues in the Treasure Valley.

Address: 516 S 9th St, Boise, ID 8370

8.4 LOCAL MARKETS AND ARTISANAL SHOPS: DISCOVERING BOISE'S CREATIVITY

From bustling farmers markets to charming artisanal shops, Boise offers numerous opportunities to discover unique, handcrafted goods and locally made products. Whether you're searching for one-of-a-kind gifts, fresh produce, or simply want to support local businesses, exploring Boise's local markets and artisanal shops is a rewarding experience. Here's a guide to some of the best places to discover Boise's creativity.

1. BOISE FARMERS MARKET

- **Overview**: The Boise Farmers Market is a beloved community hub that offers a wide variety of fresh, locally grown produce, artisanal foods, and handmade crafts. Held every Saturday from April through December, this market is a must-visit for anyone looking to experience the best of Boise's local food and craft scene.

- **What to Expect**: The market features dozens of vendors selling everything from organic vegetables and fruits to homemade jams, breads, cheeses, and baked goods. In addition to food, the market also offers a selection of handmade crafts, including pottery, jewelry, and textiles. Live music and food trucks add to the festive atmosphere.

- **Why It's Special**: The Boise Farmers Market emphasizes sustainable practices and supports small-scale, local producers. It's a great place to meet the makers, learn about their products, and enjoy a morning of shopping in a lively, community-focused setting.

- **Location**: 1500 Shoreline Dr, Boise, ID 83702

- **Hours**: Saturdays, 9:00 AM to 1:00 PM (April through December)

2. CAPITAL CITY PUBLIC MARKET

- **Overview**: Located in the heart of downtown Boise, the Capital City Public Market is another popular farmers market that showcases the creativity and talent of local artisans. Operating from April through December, this market offers a vibrant mix of food, crafts, and entertainment.

- **What to Expect**: The market features a diverse array of vendors selling fresh produce, flowers, specialty foods, and handmade crafts. From unique jewelry and clothing to original art and home décor, the Capital City Public Market is a treasure trove of local creativity. The market also hosts live music, cooking demonstrations, and special events throughout the season.

- **Why It's Special**: The Capital City Public Market is a bustling, energetic space where you can find unique, locally made products while enjoying the vibrant atmosphere of downtown Boise. It's a great place to support local artisans and find truly special items.

- **Location**: 8th Street between Bannock and Main, Boise, ID 83702

- **Hours**: Saturdays, 9:30 AM to 1:30 PM (April through December)

3. THE MAKER'S MARKET AT JUMP BOISE

- **Overview**: JUMP Boise (Jack's Urban Meeting Place) is a creative center that fosters innovation, learning, and community engagement. The Maker's Market at JUMP is a seasonal market that showcases local artisans and makers, offering a platform for them to sell their handcrafted goods.

- **What to Expect**: The Maker's Market features a curated selection of vendors selling a variety of handmade items, including jewelry, ceramics, candles, clothing, and more. The market is held in the unique and vibrant setting of JUMP, which adds to the creative and inspiring atmosphere.

- **Why It's Special**: The Maker's Market at JUMP is more than just a place to shop—it's an opportunity to connect with Boise's creative community and discover the stories behind the products. The market also often includes workshops, demonstrations, and other interactive activities.

- **Location**: 1000 W Myrtle St, Boise, ID 83702

- **Hours**: Check JUMP Boise's website for market dates and times.

4. FLYING M COFFEEHOUSE

- **Overview**: Flying M Coffeehouse is a beloved Boise institution that combines great coffee with a strong commitment to supporting local artists and makers. The coffeehouse is known for its eclectic, artsy vibe and its in-house shop, which offers a curated selection of handmade goods.

- **What to Expect**: In addition to serving up delicious coffee and baked goods, Flying M features a small retail space filled with unique, locally made products. You'll find everything from quirky art prints and handcrafted jewelry to locally made candles, ceramics, and more. The coffeehouse also hosts art shows and events, making it a lively cultural hub.

- **Why It's Special**: Flying M Coffeehouse is a perfect example of Boise's creative spirit, blending great coffee with a love for local art and culture. It's a great spot to relax, enjoy a cup of coffee, and shop for unique, locally made gifts.

- **Location**: 500 W Idaho St, Boise, ID 83702

- **Hours**: Monday to Saturday, 6:30 AM to 9:00 PM; Sunday, 7:00 AM to 7:00 PM

5. BOISE ART GLASS

- **Overview**: Boise Art Glass is a glassblowing studio and gallery where visitors can watch live glassblowing demonstrations, take classes, and shop for stunning handmade glass art. Founded by master glassblower Filip Vogelpohl, the studio is a showcase of the artistry and craftsmanship that goes into creating beautiful glass pieces.

- **What to Expect**: The gallery at Boise Art Glass features an impressive collection of glass art, including vases, bowls, jewelry, and decorative pieces. Visitors can also sign up for glassblowing classes, where they can learn the basics of this ancient art form and create their own glass pieces to take home.

- **Why It's Special**: Boise Art Glass offers a unique opportunity to experience the art of glassblowing up close and personal. The studio's combination of live demonstrations, hands-on workshops, and a gallery of exquisite glass art makes it a must-visit for art lovers and those looking to discover something truly special.

- **Location**: 1124 W Front St, Boise, ID 83702

- **Hours**: Monday to Saturday, 10:00 AM to 6:00 PM; Sunday, 11:00 AM to 5:00 PM

6. BRICOLAGE

- **Overview**: Bricolage is a locally owned boutique in downtown Boise that specializes in handmade goods, art, and creative supplies. The shop is known for its carefully curated selection of products from local artists and makers, making it a go-to destination for unique, one-of-a-kind items.

- **What to Expect**: Bricolage offers a wide range of products, including art prints, greeting cards, home décor, jewelry, and clothing. The shop also sells art supplies and DIY kits for those looking to get creative themselves. Bricolage frequently hosts art shows, workshops, and other events that celebrate local creativity.

- **Why It's Special**: Bricolage is more than just a shop—it's a community space that supports and celebrates local artists. The store's commitment to showcasing handmade, high-quality products makes it a favorite among Boise's creative crowd.

- **Location**: 418 S 6th St, Boise, ID 83702

- **Hours**: Tuesday to Saturday, 11:00 AM to 6:00 PM; Sunday, 11:00 AM to 4:00 PM

7. FREAK ALLEY GALLERY

- **Overview**: While not a traditional shop, Freak Alley Gallery is an outdoor public art gallery and a prime example of Boise's creative spirit. Located in an alleyway in downtown Boise, this ever-changing gallery features large-scale murals and street art by local and regional artists.

- **What to Expect**: Visitors to Freak Alley can stroll through the alley and admire the vibrant, colorful murals that cover the walls. The artwork ranges from abstract designs to detailed portraits, each piece telling its own story. The gallery is free and open to the public, and the murals are regularly updated, so there's always something new to see.

- **Why It's Special**: Freak Alley Gallery is a testament to Boise's thriving street art scene and the city's commitment to public art. It's a unique, open-air gallery that showcases the creativity of local artists and adds a dynamic, artistic flair to the downtown area.

- **Location**: 210 N 9th St, Boise, ID 83702

- **Hours**: Open 24/7, free to the public

8. THE DISTRICT COFFEE HOUSE

- **Overview**: The District Coffee House is a popular Boise café known for its cozy atmosphere, excellent coffee, and support for local artists and makers. In addition to serving as a gathering place for the community, The District features a small shop area where visitors can purchase locally made goods.

- **What to Expect**: The District offers a curated selection of products from local artisans, including handmade jewelry, art prints, pottery, and more. The café frequently rotates the items on display, giving different artists and makers the opportunity to showcase their work. The District also hosts art shows and live music events, making it a vibrant cultural spot.

- **Why It's Special**: The District Coffee House combines great coffee with a strong commitment to supporting local creativity. It's a welcoming space where you can relax, enjoy a cup of coffee, and discover unique, handmade products that reflect the talent and artistry of Boise's creative community.

- **Location**: 219 N 10th St, Boise, ID 83702

- **Hours**: Monday to Friday, 7:00 AM to 6:00 PM; Saturday and Sunday, 8:00 AM to 6:00 PM

9. REDISCOVERED BOOKS

- **Overview**: Rediscovered Books is an independent bookstore in downtown Boise that not only offers a wide selection of books but also supports local authors and artisans. The store is a cultural hub where book lovers can discover new titles, attend author events, and shop for locally made literary-themed gifts.

- **What to Expect**: In addition to its extensive collection of books, Rediscovered Books features a selection of locally made items, such as bookmarks, journals, tote bags, and art prints. The store frequently hosts book signings, readings, and workshops, making it a lively and engaging space for the community.

- **Why It's Special**: Rediscovered Books is more than just a bookstore—it's a place where Boise's literary and creative communities come together. The store's commitment to supporting local authors and artisans makes it a beloved destination for book lovers and anyone interested in discovering unique, handcrafted items.

- **Location**: 180 N 8th St, Boise, ID 83702

- **Hours**: Monday to Saturday, 10:00 AM to 8:00 PM; Sunday, 11:00 AM to 6:00 PM

CHAPTER 9: ACCOMMODATION GUIDE
9.1 LUXURY HOTELS AND BOUTIQUE STAYS

From upscale hotels with world-class amenities to charming boutique stays with personalized service, Boise's top accommodations provide comfort, style, and a taste of the city's unique character. Here's a guide to some of the best luxury hotels and boutique stays in Boise, complete with details on cost, pros, cons, and addresses.

1. THE GROVE HOTEL

- **Overview**: The Grove Hotel is Boise's premier luxury hotel, offering elegant accommodations, upscale amenities, and a prime downtown location. As the only AAA Four Diamond hotel in Boise, The Grove provides a sophisticated and comfortable stay for both business and leisure travelers.

- **Cost**: Rates typically range from $180 to $350 per night, depending on room type and season.

- **Pros**:

  - **Location**: Situated in the heart of downtown Boise, The Grove Hotel is within walking distance of restaurants, shops, and cultural attractions.

  - **Amenities**: The hotel features a full-service spa, fitness center, indoor pool, and on-site dining at Trillium Restaurant. Guests can also enjoy access to The Grove's rooftop terrace with stunning city views.

  - **Service**: Known for its excellent customer service, The Grove Hotel offers personalized attention and a range of concierge services.

- **Cons**:

  - **Price**: The Grove Hotel is one of the more expensive options in Boise, which may not be suitable for budget-conscious travelers.

  - **Parking**: Valet parking is available but comes with an additional fee, which some guests might find inconvenient.

- **Address**: 245 S Capitol Blvd, Boise, ID 83702

2. INN AT 500 CAPITOL

- **Overview**: The Inn at 500 Capitol is a luxury boutique hotel known for its stylish décor, personalized service, and central location. Each room is uniquely decorated with a focus on comfort and modern amenities, making it a favorite among discerning travelers.

- **Cost**: Rates typically range from $200 to $400 per night, depending on room type and season.

- **Pros**:

  - **Customization**: Guests can choose from a variety of themed rooms, each designed with a unique aesthetic and equipped with luxury amenities.

  - **Service**: The hotel offers a high level of personalized service, including complimentary valet parking, welcome drinks, and in-room dining from the on-site Richard's Restaurant.

  - **Location**: Located just steps from the Idaho State Capitol and downtown Boise's attractions, the hotel is ideal for exploring the city.

- **Cons**:

  - **Price**: As a luxury boutique hotel, the Inn at 500 Capitol is priced on the higher end, which may not be ideal for all travelers.

  - **Limited Rooms**: With a smaller number of rooms compared to larger hotels, availability may be limited during peak seasons.

- **Address**: 500 S Capitol Blvd, Boise, ID 83702

3. HOTEL 43

- **Overview**: Hotel 43 is a chic boutique hotel that combines modern design with comfort and convenience. Located in downtown Boise, the hotel offers a stylish stay with easy access to the city's top attractions, dining, and nightlife.

- **Cost**: Rates typically range from $150 to $300 per night, depending on room type and season.

- **Pros**:

  - **Design**: The hotel's contemporary décor, featuring local art and sleek furnishings, creates a stylish and inviting atmosphere.

  - **Dining**: Hotel 43 is home to Chandlers, one of Boise's top-rated steakhouses, offering fine dining and an extensive wine list.

  - **Location**: The hotel's central location makes it easy to explore downtown Boise, with many attractions just a short walk away.

- **Cons**:

  - **Limited Amenities**: While Hotel 43 offers a comfortable and stylish stay, it lacks some of the extensive amenities (such as a spa or pool) that other luxury hotels might provide.

  - **Noise**: Being in the heart of downtown, some guests might experience noise from nearby streets and nightlife, though this is generally minimal.

- **Address**: 981 W Grove St, Boise, ID 83702

4. THE MODERN HOTEL

- **Overview**: The Modern Hotel is a trendy boutique hotel housed in a mid-century modern building that has been thoughtfully renovated. Known for its minimalist design and artistic touches, The Modern offers a unique and hip experience in Boise's Linen District.

- **Cost**: Rates typically range from $130 to $250 per night, depending on room type and season.

- **Pros**:

  - **Atmosphere**: The Modern's design is sleek and contemporary, with a focus on comfort and simplicity. The hotel also features a lively bar and restaurant that draws locals and guests alike.

  - **Outdoor Space**: Guests can enjoy the hotel's outdoor courtyard, which features a fire pit and comfortable seating—perfect for relaxing after a day of exploring.

  - **Cultural Events**: The Modern frequently hosts cultural events, such as art shows, film screenings, and live music, adding to the vibrant community vibe.

- **Cons**:

  - **Room Size**: Some rooms at The Modern are on the smaller side, which might not be ideal for travelers who prefer more space.

  - **Limited Amenities**: While The Modern offers a great atmosphere and design, it lacks some of the amenities (such as a gym or spa) that other luxury hotels might offer.

- **Address**: 1314 W Grove St, Boise, ID 83702

5. RIVERSIDE HOTEL

- **Overview**: The Riverside Hotel is a full-service resort-style hotel located along the scenic Boise River. With extensive amenities, including multiple dining options, a pool, and a large outdoor event space, the Riverside Hotel offers a relaxing retreat just minutes from downtown Boise.

- **Cost**: Rates typically range from $160 to $280 per night, depending on room type and season.

- **Pros**:

  - **Location**: The hotel's riverside location offers easy access to the Boise River Greenbelt, making it ideal for outdoor enthusiasts. It's also a short drive from downtown Boise.

  - **Amenities**: The Riverside Hotel boasts a range of amenities, including a heated outdoor pool, hot tub, fitness center, and live entertainment at the on-site Sapphire Room.

  - **Family-Friendly**: With spacious rooms, a large pool, and family-friendly dining options, the Riverside Hotel is a great choice for families.

- **Cons**:

  - **Distance from Downtown**: While the hotel is close to downtown Boise, it's not within walking distance, which might be a drawback for those looking to explore the city on foot.

  - **Older Property**: The hotel is well-maintained, but some areas may show signs of age, which could be a consideration for those seeking the newest or most modern accommodations.

- **Address**: 2900 W Chinden Blvd, Boise, ID 83714

6. HYATT PLACE BOISE/DOWNTOWN

- **Overview**: Hyatt Place Boise/Downtown is a contemporary hotel offering modern accommodations and convenient amenities in the heart of Boise. It's an excellent choice for both business and leisure travelers seeking a comfortable, upscale stay with all the conveniences of a larger hotel brand.

- **Cost**: Rates typically range from $140 to $270 per night, depending on room type and season.

- **Pros**:

  - **Location**: Located downtown, the Hyatt Place is within walking distance of Boise's main attractions, including the Idaho State Capitol, local restaurants, and shopping areas.

  - **Amenities**: The hotel offers a range of amenities, including a 24/7 fitness center, an outdoor pool, complimentary breakfast, and a 24-hour gallery menu for convenient dining.

  - **Spacious Rooms**: The rooms are designed with comfort in mind, featuring separate living and sleeping areas, making them ideal for longer stays or travelers who appreciate extra space.

- **Cons**:

  - **Chain Hotel Feel**: While the Hyatt Place offers reliable quality and service, it may lack the unique character and personalized experience of some of Boise's boutique hotels.

  - **Breakfast**: Some guests have noted that the complimentary breakfast, while convenient, can get busy, leading to limited seating and food options during peak times.

- **Address**: 1024 W Bannock St, Boise, ID 83702

7. OXFORD SUITES BOISE

- **Overview**: Oxford Suites Boise is a luxury all-suite hotel that offers spacious accommodations and a range of amenities, making it an excellent choice for families, business travelers, and extended stays. The hotel is located in Boise's West End, close to shopping and dining options.

- **Cost**: Rates typically range from $150 to $260 per night, depending on room type and season.

- **Pros**:

    ○ **Spacious Suites**: Each suite offers a separate living area, kitchenettes, and large bathrooms, providing plenty of space and comfort for extended stays or families.

    ○ **Amenities**: The hotel features an indoor pool, fitness center, complimentary breakfast, and evening receptions with snacks and drinks. There's also a 24-hour business center and meeting spaces for corporate travelers.

    ○ **Value**: Oxford Suites offers a great balance of luxury and value, with amenities and spacious rooms that are often more affordable than comparable hotels.

- **Cons**:

    ○ **Location**: While the hotel is conveniently located near shopping and dining in the West End, it's a bit farther from downtown Boise, which might be a drawback for those wanting to be in the heart of the city.

    ○ **Chain Hotel Atmosphere**: Like the Hyatt Place, Oxford Suites is part of a larger chain, so it may not offer the boutique experience or local character that some travelers seek.

- **Address**: 1426 S Entertainment Ave, Boise, ID 83709

9.2 BUDGET-FRIENDLY ACCOMMODATIONS

1. RED LION HOTEL BOISE DOWNTOWNER

- **Overview**: The Red Lion Hotel Boise Downtowner is an affordable option that provides comfortable accommodations close to downtown Boise. With easy access to the city's attractions, this hotel is ideal for budget-conscious travelers looking for convenience and value.

- **Cost**: Rates typically range from $90 to $150 per night, depending on room type and season.

- **Pros**:

  - **Location**: The hotel is just a short drive or walk from downtown Boise, making it easy to explore the city's restaurants, shops, and cultural attractions.

  - **Amenities**: The Red Lion offers a range of amenities, including a seasonal outdoor pool, fitness center, free Wi-Fi, and complimentary breakfast.

  - **Pet-Friendly**: The hotel is pet-friendly, making it a great choice for travelers with pets.

- **Cons**:

  - **Dated Décor**: Some guests have noted that the hotel's décor and furnishings are a bit dated, which might not appeal to those looking for more modern accommodations.

  - **Noise**: Due to its proximity to busy roads, some rooms may experience noise from traffic, though this is generally manageable.

- **Address**: 1800 W Fairview Ave, Boise, ID 83702

2. LA QUINTA INN & SUITES BY WYNDHAM BOISE AIRPORT

- **Overview**: La Quinta Inn & Suites by Wyndham Boise Airport offers affordable, comfortable accommodations with convenient access to Boise Airport and downtown. This hotel is well-suited for travelers who need easy airport access or a quick, budget-friendly stay.

- **Cost**: Rates typically range from $80 to $130 per night, depending on room type and season.

- **Pros**:

  o **Airport Access**: The hotel is located close to Boise Airport, making it ideal for travelers with early flights or layovers. A complimentary airport shuttle is available.

  o **Free Breakfast**: Guests can enjoy a complimentary breakfast each morning, which includes a variety of hot and cold options.

  o **Indoor Pool**: The hotel features an indoor pool and hot tub, providing a relaxing spot to unwind after a day of travel or sightseeing.

- **Cons**:

  o **Limited Dining Options**: While the hotel is close to the airport, there are fewer dining options within walking distance, though downtown Boise is just a short drive away.

  o **Basic Amenities**: The hotel offers basic amenities, which may not appeal to travelers looking for more luxurious or extensive services.

- **Address**: 2613 S Vista Ave, Boise, ID 83705

3. MOTEL 6 BOISE - AIRPORT

- **Overview**: Motel 6 Boise - Airport is a no-frills, budget-friendly motel that provides basic accommodations for travelers looking to save on lodging costs. Its proximity to the airport and straightforward amenities make it a practical choice for budget travelers.

- **Cost**: Rates typically range from $60 to $90 per night, depending on room type and season.

- **Pros**:

  - **Affordability**: Motel 6 is one of the most affordable options in Boise, making it ideal for travelers on a tight budget.

  - **Pet-Friendly**: The motel is pet-friendly, and pets stay free, which is a great perk for travelers with furry companions.

  - **Location**: The motel is conveniently located near Boise Airport, with easy access to the freeway and a short drive to downtown.

- **Cons**:

  - **Basic Accommodations**: The motel offers very basic accommodations with minimal amenities, which may not be suitable for those seeking more comfort or services.

  - **Noise**: Some guests have reported noise from nearby traffic and airport activity, which could be a concern for light sleepers.

- **Address**: 2323 Airport Way, Boise, ID 83705

4. BUDGET INN BOISE

- **Overview**: Budget Inn Boise offers simple, clean, and affordable accommodations just a short drive from downtown Boise. This motel provides the essentials for a comfortable stay without the frills, making it a great option for budget travelers.

- **Cost**: Rates typically range from $70 to $110 per night, depending on room type and season.

- **Pros**:

  - **Affordability**: Budget Inn Boise is one of the more affordable options in the city, offering good value for travelers on a budget.

  - **Free Parking**: The motel offers free on-site parking, which is convenient for those traveling by car.

  - **Basic Amenities**: Rooms include essential amenities such as free Wi-Fi, cable TV, a microwave, and a mini-fridge.

- **Cons**:

  - **Older Property**: The motel is an older property, and while it's well-maintained, some guests may find the décor and furnishings outdated.

  - **Limited Services**: As a budget motel, the services and amenities are minimal, which might not meet the needs of travelers looking for more comprehensive offerings.

- **Address**: 2600 W Fairview Ave, Boise, ID 83702

5. HOLIDAY INN EXPRESS BOISE-UNIVERSITY AREA

- **Overview**: The Holiday Inn Express Boise-University Area is a budget-friendly hotel offering modern amenities and comfortable accommodations near Boise State University. It's a great option for visitors to the university or those looking to stay close to downtown.

- **Cost**: Rates typically range from $100 to $150 per night, depending on room type and season.

- **Pros**:

- **Location**: The hotel is conveniently located near Boise State University, the Greenbelt, and downtown Boise, making it easy to explore the city.

- **Free Breakfast**: Guests can enjoy a complimentary hot breakfast each morning, which includes a variety of options.

- **Modern Amenities**: The hotel offers a range of amenities, including free Wi-Fi, a fitness center, and an outdoor pool, providing good value for the price.

- **Cons**:

  - **Noise**: Some rooms may experience noise from nearby roads or university events, though this is typically manageable.

  - **Parking**: While parking is free, the lot can get busy during peak times, which may be an inconvenience for guests.

- **Address**: 475 W Parkcenter Blvd, Boise, ID 83706

6. FAIRFIELD INN BOISE

- **Overview**: Fairfield Inn Boise offers reliable, budget-friendly accommodations with a convenient location near the Boise Airport and a short drive from downtown. It's a solid choice for travelers seeking comfort and value.

- **Cost**: Rates typically range from $90 to $140 per night, depending on room type and season.

- **Pros**:

  - **Airport Proximity**: The hotel's location near Boise Airport is ideal for travelers needing quick access to flights. A complimentary airport shuttle is available.

- Free Breakfast: Guests can start their day with a complimentary hot breakfast, including eggs, waffles, fruit, and more.

- Consistent Quality: As part of the Marriott brand, Fairfield Inn offers consistent service and amenities, ensuring a comfortable stay.

- **Cons**:

  - Basic Rooms: While comfortable, the rooms are fairly standard and may lack the charm or uniqueness of more boutique options.

  - Limited Dining Options Nearby: While there are some restaurants nearby, guests may need to drive downtown for a wider variety of dining options.

- **Address**: 3300 S Shoshone St, Boise, ID 83705

7. CABANA INN BOISE

- **Overview**: Cabana Inn Boise is a locally owned budget motel located close to downtown Boise. This motel offers clean and simple accommodations with easy access to the city's attractions.

- **Cost**: Rates typically range from $60 to $100 per night, depending on room type and season.

- **Pros**:

  - Affordability: Cabana Inn offers very affordable rates, making it one of the best budget options in Boise.

  - Location: The motel is conveniently located near downtown Boise, allowing guests to explore the city without needing a car.

- ○ **Free Wi-Fi**: The motel offers free Wi-Fi in all rooms, providing guests with basic connectivity.

- **Cons**:

  - ○ **Basic Amenities**: The motel offers minimal amenities, which may not appeal to those looking for more comfort or services.

  - ○ **Dated Décor**: The property is older, and some guests may find the décor and furnishings outdated.

- **Address**: 1600 W Main St, Boise, ID 83702

8. EXTENDED STAY AMERICA - BOISE - AIRPORT

- **Overview**: Extended Stay America - Boise - Airport offers budget-friendly, extended-stay accommodations with fully equipped kitchens, making it a great choice for longer stays or travelers who prefer to cook their own meals.

- **Cost**: Rates typically range from $80 to $120 per night, with discounts often available for longer stays.

- **Pros**:

  - ○ **Kitchens**: Each suite includes a fully equipped kitchen with a stove, microwave, refrigerator, and utensils, ideal for guests who want to prepare their own meals.

  - ○ **Extended-Stay Discounts**: The hotel offers discounts for longer stays, making it a cost-effective option for extended visits to Boise.

  - ○ **Pet-Friendly**: The hotel is pet-friendly, allowing guests to bring their pets along for an additional fee.

- **Cons**:

- - **Limited Housekeeping**: Housekeeping services are limited, which may not appeal to guests who prefer daily room cleaning.

  - **Basic Amenities**: The hotel offers essential amenities, but lacks some of the features (like a pool or fitness center) that other hotels might provide.

- **Address**: 2500 S Vista Ave, Boise, ID 83705

9.3 FAMILY-FRIENDLY LODGING OPTIONS

1. HOMEWOOD SUITES BY HILTON BOISE

- **Overview**: Homewood Suites by Hilton Boise is a great option for families looking for spacious accommodations with all the comforts of home. The hotel offers suite-style rooms with full kitchens, making it ideal for families who prefer to prepare their own meals or need extra space.

- **Cost**: Rates typically range from $150 to $250 per night, depending on room type and season.

- **Pros**:

  - **Spacious Suites**: Each suite includes a separate living area, full kitchen, and multiple sleeping options, providing plenty of space for families.

  - **Complimentary Breakfast and Evening Social**: Guests can enjoy a complimentary hot breakfast each morning, and the hotel also offers an evening social with light snacks and drinks on select weekdays.

  - **Family-Friendly Amenities**: The hotel features an indoor pool, hot tub, and a game room, which are sure to keep kids entertained.

- **Cons:**

  - **Location:** While the hotel is located in a quiet area, it's a bit farther from downtown Boise, which may require driving to reach certain attractions.

  - **Price:** The rates can be higher during peak seasons, which might not be ideal for budget-conscious families.

- **Address:** 7957 W Spectrum St, Boise, ID 83709

2. OXFORD SUITES BOISE

- **Overview:** Oxford Suites Boise offers comfortable, family-friendly accommodations with a range of amenities designed to make your stay enjoyable. With spacious suites and a convenient location near shopping and dining, this hotel is perfect for families visiting Boise.

- **Cost:** Rates typically range from $150 to $260 per night, depending on room type and season.

- **Pros:**

  - **Spacious Rooms:** The suites offer ample space for families, with separate living areas and kitchenettes, making it easy to accommodate children.

  - **Complimentary Breakfast and Evening Reception:** Families can enjoy a free breakfast buffet each morning and an evening reception with snacks and drinks.

  - **Indoor Pool:** The hotel's indoor pool is a hit with kids, providing a fun way to unwind after a day of sightseeing.

- **Cons:**

  - **Distance from Downtown:** The hotel is located in Boise's West End, which is a short drive from downtown and some of the city's main attractions.

- o   **Busy During Peak Times**: The hotel can get busy during peak travel seasons, which might affect the availability of amenities like the pool and breakfast area.

- **Address**: 1426 S Entertainment Ave, Boise, ID 83709

3. SPRINGHILL SUITES BY MARRIOTT BOISE PARKCENTER

- **Overview**: SpringHill Suites by Marriott Boise ParkCenter offers modern, family-friendly accommodations with spacious suites and easy access to Boise's attractions. The hotel's location near the Boise River Greenbelt makes it a great choice for active families who enjoy outdoor activities.

- **Cost**: Rates typically range from $130 to $220 per night, depending on room type and season.

- **Pros**:

  - o   **Spacious Suites**: The hotel's suites include separate living areas, sofa beds, and kitchenettes, providing plenty of room for families.

  - o   **Proximity to Outdoor Activities**: The hotel is located near the Boise River Greenbelt, offering easy access to walking and biking trails, parks, and other outdoor attractions.

  - o   **Complimentary Breakfast**: Families can start the day with a free hot breakfast, including a variety of options to suit different tastes.

- **Cons**:

  - o   **Limited On-Site Dining**: The hotel does not have a full-service restaurant, though there are several dining options nearby.

    ○ **Pool Size**: While the hotel has an outdoor pool, it may be smaller than what some families are looking for, especially during busy times.

- **Address**: 424 E Parkcenter Blvd, Boise, ID 83706

4. HYATT PLACE BOISE/DOWNTOWN

- **Overview**: Hyatt Place Boise/Downtown is a family-friendly hotel located in the heart of Boise, offering modern accommodations and convenient access to the city's top attractions. The hotel's central location makes it easy to explore Boise's museums, parks, and dining options.

- **Cost**: Rates typically range from $140 to $270 per night, depending on room type and season.

- **Pros**:

    ○ **Central Location**: The hotel's downtown location puts families within walking distance of many attractions, including the Idaho State Capitol, Zoo Boise, and the Boise Art Museum.

    ○ **Spacious Rooms**: The rooms are designed with families in mind, featuring separate sleeping and living areas, sofa beds, and mini-fridges.

    ○ **Complimentary Breakfast**: A free hot breakfast is available each morning, with a variety of kid-friendly options.

- **Cons**:

    ○ **Limited On-Site Dining**: While the hotel offers a 24/7 gallery menu, there is no full-service restaurant on-site. However, plenty of dining options are available nearby.

- o **Parking Fees**: The hotel charges for parking, which can add to the overall cost of the stay.

- **Address**: 1024 W Bannock St, Boise, ID 83702

5. HAMPTON INN & SUITES BOISE-DOWNTOWN

- **Overview**: The Hampton Inn & Suites Boise-Downtown is a popular choice for families, offering comfortable accommodations and a convenient downtown location. With family-friendly amenities and easy access to Boise's attractions, this hotel is a great option for those visiting the city with kids.

- **Cost**: Rates typically range from $140 to $250 per night, depending on room type and season.

- **Pros**:

  - o **Location**: The hotel is located in the heart of downtown Boise, close to popular attractions like the Boise Zoo, Discovery Center of Idaho, and the Basque Block.

  - o **Indoor Pool**: The hotel's indoor pool and hot tub are perfect for families looking to relax and have fun.

  - o **Complimentary Breakfast**: Guests can enjoy a free hot breakfast each morning, with options that appeal to both kids and adults.

- **Cons**:

  - o **Parking Fees**: The hotel charges for parking, which may be a consideration for budget-conscious families.

  - o **Busy During Peak Times**: The hotel's downtown location can make it busy during peak travel seasons, which might affect the availability of amenities like the pool and breakfast area.

- **Address**: 495 S Capitol Blvd, Boise, ID 83702

6. RESIDENCE INN BY MARRIOTT BOISE DOWNTOWN/UNIVERSITY

- **Overview**: The Residence Inn by Marriott Boise Downtown/University offers spacious suites with full kitchens, making it an excellent choice for families planning longer stays or those who prefer the convenience of cooking their own meals. The hotel's location near Boise State University and the Greenbelt is ideal for families who enjoy outdoor activities.

- **Cost**: Rates typically range from $150 to $250 per night, depending on room type and season.

- **Pros**:

    - **Spacious Suites with Kitchens**: The suites feature full kitchens, separate living areas, and multiple sleeping options, providing ample space and convenience for families.

    - **Outdoor Pool and Sports Court**: The hotel offers an outdoor pool, hot tub, and sports court, giving kids plenty of opportunities for fun and exercise.

    - **Complimentary Breakfast**: A hot breakfast is included, with options to suit all tastes.

- **Cons**:

    - **Limited On-Site Dining**: The hotel does not have a full-service restaurant, though the in-room kitchens and nearby dining options make up for this.

    - **Distance from Downtown**: While the hotel is close to Boise State University, it's a bit farther from downtown Boise's main attractions, though still within a short drive.

- **Address**: 1401 S Lusk Pl, Boise, ID 83706

7. TOWNEPLACE SUITES BY MARRIOTT BOISE DOWNTOWN/UNIVERSITY

- **Overview**: TownePlace Suites by Marriott Boise Downtown/University offers comfortable, family-friendly accommodations with suite-style rooms and convenient amenities. The hotel is close to Boise State University and downtown Boise, making it a great base for exploring the city.

- **Cost**: Rates typically range from $130 to $220 per night, depending on room type and season.

- **Pros**:

  o **Suites with Kitchens**: Each suite includes a fully equipped kitchen, making it easy for families to prepare meals and snacks.

  o **Outdoor Pool**: The hotel's outdoor pool is perfect for families looking to relax and cool off after a day of sightseeing.

  o **Complimentary Breakfast**: A free breakfast buffet is available each morning, offering a variety of options to start the day.

- **Cons**:

  o **Limited Dining Options Nearby**: While the hotel is close to Boise State University, there are fewer dining options within walking distance, though downtown Boise is a short drive away.

  o **Basic Amenities**: The hotel offers essential amenities, but may lack some of the features (like a game room or larger pool) that other family-friendly hotels provide.

- **Address**: 1455 S Capitol Blvd, Boise, ID 83706

8. HOLIDAY INN EXPRESS BOISE-UNIVERSITY AREA

- **Overview**: Holiday Inn Express Boise-University Area is a budget-friendly, family-oriented hotel offering modern amenities and a convenient location near Boise State University and the Greenbelt. It's a great choice for families looking for affordability and comfort.

- **Cost**: Rates typically range from $100 to $150 per night, depending on room type and season.

- **Pros**:

  - **Location**: The hotel's location near Boise State University and the Greenbelt provides easy access to outdoor activities and downtown attractions.

  - **Complimentary Breakfast**: Guests can enjoy a free hot breakfast each morning, with a variety of options for both kids and adults.

  - **Indoor Pool**: The hotel features an indoor pool, which is perfect for families looking to relax and have fun.

- **Cons**:

  - **Noise**: Some rooms may experience noise from nearby roads or university events, though this is typically manageable.

  - **Limited On-Site Dining**: While there are some dining options nearby, the hotel itself does not have a full-service restaurant.

- **Address**: 475 W Parkcenter Blvd, Boise, ID 83706

9.4 TIPS FOR BOOKING AND STAYING

Booking and staying in Boise can be a smooth and enjoyable experience with the right preparation. Whether you're visiting for a short trip or an extended stay, these tips will help you make the most of your visit, from choosing the right accommodation to exploring the city's attractions.

1. BOOK EARLY FOR BEST RATES AND AVAILABILITY

- **Plan Ahead**: Boise is a popular destination, especially during peak travel seasons, such as summer, holidays, and during major events like the Treefort Music Fest. Booking your accommodation well in advance ensures you get the best rates and a wider selection of rooms.

- **Flexible Dates**: If your travel dates are flexible, consider adjusting your stay by a few days to take advantage of lower rates. Midweek stays often cost less than weekends.

- **Use Price Comparison Tools**: Websites and apps like Google Hotel Search, Booking.com, or Expedia can help you compare prices across different accommodations. Be sure to check if booking directly through the hotel offers any additional perks or discounts.

2. CHOOSE THE RIGHT LOCATION

- **Proximity to Attractions**: Consider what you want to do in Boise and choose your accommodation accordingly. If you're interested in exploring downtown Boise, staying in the city center or nearby can save you time and transportation costs. For outdoor activities, consider lodging closer to the Boise River Greenbelt or the Boise Foothills.

- **Transportation Access**: If you're planning to explore areas outside of downtown, such as Bogus Basin or the Boise National Forest, make sure your accommodation has convenient access to major roads or public transportation.

3. CONSIDER FAMILY-FRIENDLY OR PET-FRIENDLY OPTIONS

- **Family-Friendly Amenities**: If you're traveling with children, look for hotels that offer family-friendly amenities such as spacious suites, kitchenettes, pools, and complimentary breakfast. Some hotels also provide cribs, high chairs, and kids' activities.

- **Pet-Friendly Accommodations**: Many Boise hotels and motels are pet-friendly, but policies and fees can vary. Be sure to confirm the pet policy when booking and inquire about nearby parks or pet-friendly areas.

4. CHECK FOR DEALS AND PACKAGES

- **Special Offers**: Many hotels offer special packages, such as romantic getaways, adventure packages, or extended-stay discounts. These can include perks like complimentary meals, tickets to local attractions, or discounts on activities.

- **Membership Discounts**: If you're a member of AAA, AARP, or a loyalty program, you may be eligible for discounts on your stay. Always check if your memberships or affiliations offer any benefits.

- **Group Bookings**: If you're traveling with a group, inquire about group rates or discounts for multiple rooms. Some hotels offer packages specifically for weddings, reunions, or corporate events.

5. READ REVIEWS AND RESEARCH

- **Check Reviews**: Before booking, read reviews from other travelers on platforms like TripAdvisor, Yelp, or Google Reviews. Look for recent reviews to get an accurate picture of the property's current condition and service.

- **Research Amenities**: Make sure the accommodation offers the amenities you need, such as free Wi-Fi, parking, a fitness center, or a business center. If you have specific needs, such as accessibility features, call the hotel directly to confirm availability.

6. CONSIDER ALTERNATIVE ACCOMMODATIONS

- **Vacation Rentals**: For longer stays or larger groups, vacation rentals through platforms like Airbnb or Vrbo can offer more space and amenities like full kitchens and laundry facilities. This can be a cost-effective option, especially if you plan to cook your own meals.

- **Extended-Stay Hotels**: If you're staying in Boise for an extended period, consider an extended-stay hotel that offers apartment-style accommodations with kitchens and living areas. These properties often offer discounts for longer stays.

7. BE AWARE OF EXTRA FEES

- **Parking Fees**: Some downtown hotels charge for parking, which can add to the cost of your stay. Be sure to factor in any additional fees when comparing accommodations.

- **Resort Fees**: Some hotels may charge a resort fee that covers amenities like pools, gyms, or Wi-Fi. Always check the fine print to avoid surprises at checkout.

- **Cancellation Policies**: Understand the hotel's cancellation policy before booking, especially if your plans are subject to change. Flexible booking options might come with higher rates but offer peace of mind.

8. PACK APPROPRIATELY FOR BOISE'S CLIMATE

- **Layered Clothing**: Boise has a semi-arid climate with hot summers and cold winters. Pack layers to adjust to varying temperatures, especially if you plan to spend time outdoors.

- **Comfortable Shoes**: Whether you're exploring downtown or hiking in the foothills, comfortable walking shoes are a must.

- **Sun Protection**: Boise enjoys plenty of sunshine year-round, so bring sunscreen, sunglasses, and a hat to protect yourself during outdoor activities.

9. EXPLORE LOCAL DINING AND ENTERTAINMENT

- **Local Cuisine**: Boise is known for its farm-to-table dining and craft beer scene. Ask your hotel for recommendations on local restaurants and breweries, or explore Boise's famous Basque Block for a taste of the city's unique heritage.

- **Entertainment and Events**: Check local event calendars for festivals, live music, and cultural events during your stay. Boise has a vibrant arts scene, and there's always something happening around town.

10. BE MINDFUL OF BOISE'S ETIQUETTE AND CULTURE

- **Respect the Environment**: Boise residents are proud of their city's natural beauty. Help preserve it by staying on trails, disposing of waste properly, and respecting local wildlife.

- **Tipping**: Like most places in the U.S., tipping is customary in Boise. A tip of 15-20% is standard in restaurants, and it's polite to tip hotel staff, such as housekeeping and valet, for good service.

11. TRANSPORTATION AND GETTING AROUND

- **Rental Cars**: Renting a car can give you the flexibility to explore Boise and the surrounding areas at your own pace. Most major car rental companies operate out of Boise Airport.

- **Public Transportation**: Boise's public transportation system, ValleyRide, offers bus services throughout the city. It's a convenient option if you're staying downtown and don't want to rent a car.

- **Biking and Walking**: Boise is a bike-friendly city with plenty of bike lanes and trails. Consider renting a bike to explore the Boise River Greenbelt or other nearby attractions.

12. ENJOY YOUR STAY AND EMBRACE THE LOCAL VIBE

- **Relax and Enjoy**: Boise is known for its friendly, laid-back atmosphere. Take time to enjoy the local culture, meet the residents, and explore the city's many attractions at your own pace.

- **Stay Safe**: Boise is generally a safe city, but it's always wise to take standard precautions, such as locking your car, keeping valuables secure, and being aware of your surroundings.

CHAPTER 10: ITINERARY PLANNING

10.1 CRAFTING THE PERFECT ITINERARY

Planning the perfect itinerary for your trip to Boise ensures you make the most of your time in this vibrant city. Whether you're visiting for a weekend getaway, a week-long adventure, or an extended stay, a well-crafted itinerary helps you balance sightseeing, relaxation, and exploration. Here's a detailed guide to creating the perfect Boise itinerary, tailored to different travel styles and interests.

1. KNOW YOUR INTERESTS AND PRIORITIZE ACTIVITIES

- **Identify Your Travel Style**: Before crafting your itinerary, consider your travel style. Are you an outdoor enthusiast eager to explore Boise's natural beauty? A foodie interested in local dining experiences? Or perhaps a culture lover looking to dive into the city's arts and history? Identifying your interests will help you prioritize activities.

- **Research Top Attractions**: Boise offers a wide range of attractions, from outdoor adventures in the Boise Foothills to cultural experiences in the Basque Block. Make a list of must-see sights and activities, then rank them based on your interests and the time available.

- **Balance Busy Days with Relaxation**: Ensure your itinerary includes a mix of activities and downtime. While it's tempting to pack your days with sightseeing, remember to schedule time to relax, whether it's enjoying a leisurely meal or strolling through a park.

2. CONSIDER THE LENGTH OF YOUR STAY

- **Weekend Getaway**: If you're visiting Boise for a weekend, focus on the city's highlights. A two-day itinerary might include exploring downtown Boise, visiting the Boise Art Museum, walking the Boise River Greenbelt, and enjoying a meal in the Basque Block.

- **Extended Stay**: For a longer visit, you can dive deeper into the city's offerings. Consider day trips to nearby attractions like Bogus Basin for skiing or hiking, the Idaho Botanical Garden, or the Snake River Valley for wine tasting.

- **Day-by-Day Planning**: Break your itinerary down into manageable days, with each day focusing on a specific area or theme. For example, dedicate one day to exploring downtown Boise and its cultural attractions, another to outdoor activities in the Boise Foothills, and a third to discovering the local food scene.

3. START WITH THE ESSENTIALS: DAY ONE

- **Arrival and Check-In**: Plan to arrive early enough to check into your accommodation and get settled. Depending on your arrival time, you may want to start exploring right away or relax before heading out.

- **Orientation and Exploration**: Begin your Boise adventure with a walk through downtown. Visit the Idaho State Capitol, stroll along 8th Street for shopping and dining, and get a feel for the city's vibe.

- **Evening Activity**: Cap off your first day with dinner at a local restaurant, followed by a visit to Freak Alley Gallery to admire the street art. If you're up for it, catch a live performance at one of Boise's many music venues or theaters.

4. INCORPORATE OUTDOOR ADVENTURES

- **Boise River Greenbelt**: Dedicate a morning or afternoon to exploring the Boise River Greenbelt, a 25-mile path that runs along the river and offers scenic views, parks, and wildlife. Rent a bike or simply walk, stopping at Julia Davis Park or the Anne Frank Human Rights Memorial.

- **Boise Foothills**: For hiking enthusiasts, the Boise Foothills offer trails for all levels. Start your day early with a hike up Camel's Back Park for panoramic views of the city, or tackle a more challenging trail like the Hulls Gulch Reserve.

- **Bogus Basin**: If you're visiting in winter, spend a day skiing or snowboarding at Bogus Basin. In the warmer months, the area offers hiking, mountain biking, and scenic chairlift rides.

5. EXPERIENCE BOISE'S CULTURE AND HISTORY

- **Basque Block**: Spend a morning exploring the Basque Block, learning about Boise's Basque heritage at the Basque Museum & Cultural Center. Enjoy lunch at a Basque restaurant like Bar Gernika or The Basque Market.

- **Museums and Galleries**: Visit the Boise Art Museum to see contemporary art exhibits, or head to the Idaho State Museum for an overview of the state's history. Don't miss the Discovery Center of Idaho if you're traveling with kids.

- **Historical Landmarks**: Explore Boise's historical landmarks, such as the Old Idaho Penitentiary, which offers a fascinating glimpse into the city's past. The Idaho Anne Frank Human Rights Memorial is also worth a visit for its powerful message.

6. DIVE INTO BOISE'S FOOD AND DRINK SCENE

- **Farm-to-Table Dining**: Plan a meal at one of Boise's farm-to-table restaurants, where you can enjoy fresh, locally sourced ingredients. Options include Bittercreek Alehouse, State & Lemp, or The Modern Hotel and Bar.

- **Craft Breweries**: Boise is known for its craft beer scene, so include a visit to a few local breweries in your itinerary. Stop by Payette Brewing Company, Lost Grove Brewing, or Boise Brewing for a tasting.

- **Farmers Markets**: If you're visiting on a Saturday, explore the Boise Farmers Market or the Capital City Public Market. These markets offer fresh produce, artisanal foods, and handmade crafts, providing a taste of local life.

7. PLAN FOR FAMILY-FRIENDLY ACTIVITIES

- **Zoo Boise**: Spend a morning at Zoo Boise, where kids can see animals from around the world and participate in interactive exhibits. The zoo is located in Julia Davis Park, making it easy to combine with other activities.

- **Discovery Center of Idaho**: For hands-on learning and fun, take the family to the Discovery Center of Idaho. This interactive science museum offers exhibits and activities that engage kids and adults alike.

- **Parks and Playgrounds**: Include time to explore Boise's parks, such as Ann Morrison Park or Kathryn Albertson Park. These green spaces offer playgrounds, walking trails, and picnic areas, perfect for family outings.

8. EXPLORE BEYOND BOISE: DAY TRIPS AND EXCURSIONS

- **Day Trip to Idaho City**: Take a day trip to Idaho City, a historic gold rush town about an hour from Boise. Explore the town's history, visit the Idaho City Historical Museum, and soak in the natural hot springs.

- **Snake River Valley Wine Tour**: Plan a day to visit the wineries of the Snake River Valley, just a short drive from Boise. Enjoy tastings at local vineyards, such as Ste. Chapelle Winery or Sawtooth Winery, and take in the scenic views.

- **Lucky Peak State Park**: Spend a day at Lucky Peak State Park, where you can enjoy boating, fishing, and picnicking by the reservoir. It's a great spot for outdoor relaxation and water activities.

9. Leave Room for Spontaneity

- **Flexible Time**: While it's important to have a plan, leave some time in your itinerary for spontaneous exploration. You might discover a hidden gem, like a local café, boutique, or event that wasn't on your original list.

- **Ask Locals for Recommendations**: Boiseans are known for their friendliness, so don't hesitate to ask locals for their favorite spots or activities. You might get tips on a great hiking trail, a new restaurant, or an upcoming event.

10. Final Day: Wrapping Up Your Visit

- **Last-Minute Shopping**: Use your final day to pick up souvenirs or gifts from local shops. Consider visiting the Boise Co-op or Flying M Coffeehouse for locally made products.

- **Relaxation**: After a busy trip, take some time to relax. Visit the Idaho Botanical Garden for a peaceful stroll, or enjoy a leisurely breakfast at one of Boise's popular brunch spots like Goldy's Breakfast Bistro.

- **Departure**: Plan your departure to allow time for packing, check-out, and travel to the airport or your next destination. If you have a late flight, you might squeeze in one last activity or meal before you go.

10.2 Best Time of Year to Visit

Boise, Idaho, is a destination that offers something unique and enjoyable year-round. The best time to visit depends on your interests and the type of activities you're looking to enjoy. Here's a seasonal guide to help you decide the ideal time to plan your trip to Boise.

Spring (March to May)

Why **Visit?**

Spring is one of the best times to visit Boise, especially for outdoor enthusiasts. The weather starts to warm up, flowers begin to bloom, and the city comes alive with events and activities.

Weather:

- Temperatures: Ranges from 40°F (4°C) in March to 70°F (21°C) in May.

- Mild and pleasant, with occasional rain showers.

Pros:

- **Outdoor Activities:** Spring is perfect for hiking, biking, and exploring the Boise River Greenbelt. The Boise Foothills are lush and green, offering beautiful scenery for outdoor adventures.

- **Events:** The season is filled with festivals, including the Boise Flower & Garden Show in March and the famous Treefort Music Fest in late March, which features music, film, art, and food.

- **Fewer Crowds:** While Boise is starting to wake up from winter, it's still less crowded than during the summer months.

Cons:

- **Unpredictable Weather:** Spring weather can be unpredictable, with the possibility of rain or cooler temperatures. It's wise to pack layers and be prepared for a mix of conditions.

SUMMER (JUNE TO AUGUST)

Why Visit?

Summer is peak tourist season in Boise, offering long days filled with sunshine and a packed calendar of events. It's ideal for those who enjoy outdoor activities and warm weather.

Weather:

- Temperatures: Average highs range from 80°F (27°C) in June to 90°F (32°C) in July and August.

- Warm and dry, with occasional heatwaves.

Pros:

- **Outdoor Fun:** Summer is perfect for enjoying the Boise River, whether you're rafting, kayaking, or floating. It's also the best time for hiking, camping, and visiting local parks.

- **Festivals and Events:** Boise hosts numerous summer events, including the Boise Music Festival in June, the Twilight Criterium in July, and the Boise Farmers Market every Saturday.

- **Long Days:** With extended daylight hours, you have more time to explore the city and surrounding areas.

Cons:

- **Higher Prices and Crowds:** Summer is the most popular time to visit, so accommodations and flights can be more expensive. Tourist spots and outdoor attractions may be crowded.

- **Hot Weather:** Temperatures can soar, especially in July and August, making outdoor activities uncomfortable during the hottest part of the day.

Fall (September to November)

Why Visit?

Fall is a fantastic time to visit Boise, with cooler temperatures, stunning fall foliage, and a slower pace compared to the busy summer season.

Weather:

- Temperatures: Ranges from 75°F (24°C) in September to 50°F (10°C) in November.

- Crisp and cool, with beautiful clear skies.

Pros:

- **Fall Foliage:** The changing leaves create a picturesque setting, especially in parks like Kathryn Albertson Park and along the Boise River Greenbelt.

- **Harvest Season:** Fall is a great time to visit Boise's farmers markets and enjoy seasonal produce. The city also hosts harvest festivals and wine events in the nearby Snake River Valley.

- **Comfortable Weather:** The cooler temperatures are ideal for outdoor activities without the summer heat, and it's a great time for hiking, biking, and enjoying Boise's outdoor spaces.

Cons:

- **Shorter Days:** As fall progresses, the days get shorter, which means less daylight for outdoor activities.

- **Chillier Weather:** November can bring much cooler temperatures, especially in the evenings, so be sure to pack warm clothing.

WINTER (DECEMBER TO FEBRUARY)

Why   **Visit?**
Winter in Boise is perfect for those who love winter sports, cozy atmospheres, and holiday festivities. It's a quieter time to visit, with fewer tourists and a peaceful, laid-back vibe.

Weather:

- Temperatures: Average highs range from 30°F (-1°C) to 40°F (4°C).

- Cold, with occasional snowfall, especially in the mountains.

Pros:

- **Skiing and Snowboarding:** Bogus Basin, just 16 miles from downtown Boise, offers excellent skiing, snowboarding, and tubing. It's a great winter getaway for snow lovers.

- **Holiday Spirit:** Boise's downtown lights up for the holidays, with festive events like the Winter Garden aGlow at the Idaho Botanical Garden and the Capital City Public Market's holiday market.

- **Fewer Crowds:** Winter is the off-season, so you'll find lower prices on accommodations and fewer crowds at major attractions.

Cons:

- **Cold Weather:** The cold temperatures might not appeal to everyone, especially if you prefer warmer weather for outdoor activities.

- **Limited Outdoor Activities:** Some outdoor activities, like hiking and biking, are limited in winter due to snow and colder conditions.

BEST TIME TO VISIT FOR SPECIFIC ACTIVITIES

- **For Outdoor Adventures:** Spring and fall are ideal for hiking, biking, and exploring Boise's natural beauty. The weather is mild, and the landscapes are stunning.

- **For Festivals and Events:** Summer offers the most events and festivals, including the Treefort Music Fest in spring, Boise Music Festival in summer, and various fall harvest festivals.

- **For Skiing and Snowboarding:** Winter is the best time to visit if you're interested in winter sports at Bogus Basin.

- **For Wine Tasting:** Late summer to early fall is the perfect time to explore the Snake River Valley's wineries, with harvest season offering special events and tastings.

10.3 SEASONAL ACTIVITIES AND EVENTS

SPRING (MARCH TO MAY)

Activities:

- **Hiking and Biking**: Spring is the perfect time to explore the Boise Foothills as the trails come to life with blooming wildflowers. Popular spots include Camel's Back Park, Hulls Gulch Reserve, and Table Rock.

- **Boise River Greenbelt**: Enjoy a walk or bike ride along the Boise River Greenbelt, a scenic 25-mile path that winds through parks, along the river, and offers stunning views of the surrounding landscape.

- **Gardens and Parks**: Visit the Idaho Botanical Garden to see spring blooms, or take a leisurely stroll through Julia Davis Park or Kathryn Albertson Park, where you can enjoy the fresh air and spring colors.

Events:

- **Treefort Music Fest (Late March)**: One of Boise's most popular events, Treefort Music Fest is a multi-day celebration of music, film, art, and food. The festival features hundreds of performances across various venues and "forts" dedicated to different interests, such as Storyfort, Alefort, and Comedyfort.

- **Boise Flower & Garden Show (March)**: This annual event at the Boise Centre showcases garden displays, workshops, and vendors offering everything from plants to garden art. It's a must-visit for gardening enthusiasts.

- **Freak Alley Gallery Mural Painting (April-May)**: Spring is a great time to visit Freak Alley Gallery, as new murals are often painted during this time. You can watch artists in action and see the alley's ever-changing art.

SUMMER (JUNE TO AUGUST)

Activities:

- **River Rafting and Tubing**: Cool off in the summer heat by rafting or tubing down the Boise River. You can rent equipment locally and enjoy a relaxing float with beautiful views of the city and surrounding nature.

- **Outdoor Concerts and Movies**: Boise offers numerous outdoor concerts and movie nights in the summer. Popular venues include the Idaho Botanical Garden's Outlaw Field, which hosts concerts, and local parks that feature movie nights under the stars.

- **Farmers Markets**: Explore the Boise Farmers Market and the Capital City Public Market on Saturdays to enjoy fresh produce, local crafts, and live music.

Events:

- **Boise Music Festival (June)**: Held at Expo Idaho, the Boise Music Festival is a full day of live music across multiple stages, featuring national headliners, regional acts, and local bands. The festival also includes a carnival, food vendors, and a beer garden.

- **4th of July Celebrations**: Boise celebrates Independence Day with fireworks, parades, and family-friendly activities. Ann Morrison

Park is the center of festivities, with a spectacular fireworks display to end the evening.

- **Twilight Criterium (July)**: This high-speed bike race through downtown Boise attracts top cyclists and offers an exciting spectacle for spectators. The event includes races for various categories and a fun atmosphere with food and drinks.

FALL (SEPTEMBER TO NOVEMBER)

Activities:

- **Leaf Peeping**: Fall foliage in Boise is stunning, especially in areas like the Boise River Greenbelt, Camel's Back Park, and the Boise Foothills. The golden and red leaves make for beautiful hikes and walks.

- **Wine Tasting**: Fall is harvest season in the nearby Snake River Valley, Idaho's wine country. Spend a day touring local wineries, enjoying tastings, and experiencing the region's unique terroir.

- **Pumpkin Patches and Corn Mazes**: Visit local farms like Linder Farms or The Farmstead for fall activities, including pumpkin picking, corn mazes, hayrides, and other family-friendly fun.

Events:

- **Art in the Park (September)**: Held in Julia Davis Park, this annual arts and crafts festival organized by the Boise Art Museum features hundreds of artists and artisans selling everything from paintings to pottery. The event also includes live music, food vendors, and activities for kids.

- **Hyde Park Street Fair (September)**: This community event in Boise's North End features live music, local vendors, food trucks, and family activities. It's a great way to experience Boise's vibrant local culture.

- **Oktoberfest Celebrations (October)**: Various locations around Boise host Oktoberfest events, featuring German beer, traditional food, and live music. These celebrations often include fun activities like stein-holding contests and polka dancing.

WINTER (DECEMBER TO FEBRUARY)

Activities:

- **Skiing and Snowboarding at Bogus Basin**: Just 16 miles from downtown Boise, Bogus Basin is the go-to destination for winter sports. Enjoy skiing, snowboarding, tubing, and even Nordic skiing with breathtaking views of the surrounding mountains.

- **Holiday Light Displays**: Boise gets into the festive spirit with numerous holiday light displays. Winter Garden aGlow at the Idaho Botanical Garden is a must-see, featuring over 500,000 lights. Downtown Boise also lights up with decorations and a large Christmas tree in The Grove Plaza.

- **Ice Skating**: The Village at Meridian, a short drive from Boise, offers an outdoor ice-skating rink during the winter months. It's a fun activity for families and couples alike.

Events:

- **Winter Garden aGlow (Late November to Early January)**: This annual event at the Idaho Botanical Garden transforms the garden into a winter wonderland with dazzling light displays, holiday music, and visits from Santa Claus.

- **New Year's Eve Potato Drop (December 31st)**: Boise's unique twist on the traditional New Year's Eve ball drop, the Idaho Potato Drop is a fun, family-friendly event held in front of the Idaho State Capitol. The event includes live music, food vendors, and fireworks.

- **Boise Philharmonic Holiday Concerts (December)**: The Boise Philharmonic offers several holiday-themed concerts throughout

December, including performances of classic holiday music, "The Nutcracker," and more.

YEAR-ROUND ACTIVITIES

- **Boise Art Museum**: Open year-round, the Boise Art Museum features contemporary art exhibitions, educational programs, and special events. It's a cultural hub for art lovers and offers something new with each visit.

- **Old Idaho Penitentiary**: This historical site offers tours year-round, giving visitors a glimpse into Boise's past. Special events, like spooky tours during Halloween, add an extra layer of interest.

- **Basque Block**: Boise's Basque Block is always a vibrant place to visit, offering a taste of Basque culture through its museums, restaurants, and cultural events.

10.4 RESOURCES FOR PLANNING

Planning a trip to Boise is an exciting process, and having the right resources at your disposal can make your planning smoother and more enjoyable. Whether you're looking for detailed travel guides, booking tools, local insights, or transportation options, this guide will provide you with the essential resources to plan your Boise adventure with ease.

1. TRAVEL GUIDES AND WEBSITES

- **Visit Boise (Boise Convention & Visitors Bureau)**

    - **Website**: visitboise.com

    - **Overview**: This official tourism website offers comprehensive information about Boise, including things to do, places to stay, upcoming events, and travel tips. It's a great starting point for planning your trip.

- **Resources**: Interactive maps, itinerary suggestions, event calendars, and downloadable brochures.

- **Idaho Travel Guide (Idaho Tourism)**

  - **Website**: visitidaho.org

  - **Overview**: Idaho's official travel site provides detailed information about Boise and the surrounding areas. It covers accommodations, dining, outdoor activities, and more.

  - **Resources**: Trip planning tools, scenic byways, and outdoor adventure guides.

- **TripAdvisor**

  - **Website**: tripadvisor.com

  - **Overview**: TripAdvisor offers user-generated reviews and recommendations for hotels, restaurants, and attractions in Boise. It's useful for getting a sense of what other travelers have enjoyed.

  - **Resources**: Hotel and restaurant rankings, traveler reviews, photos, and forums.

2. BOOKING ACCOMMODATIONS

- **Booking.com**

  - **Website**: booking.com

  - **Overview**: A popular platform for booking hotels, motels, and vacation rentals in Boise. It offers a wide range of options, from budget to luxury accommodations.

  - **Resources**: Filter by price, location, and amenities; read guest reviews; and compare prices.

- **Airbnb**

  - **Website**: airbnb.com

  - **Overview**: Airbnb offers unique lodging options, including homes, apartments, and boutique stays in Boise. It's a great way to find accommodations that suit your style and budget.

  - **Resources**: Search by neighborhood, property type, and price; read reviews; and contact hosts directly.

- **Expedia**

  - **Website**: expedia.com

  - **Overview**: Expedia allows you to book hotels, flights, rental cars, and vacation packages all in one place. It's a convenient resource for travelers looking to bundle services.

  - **Resources**: Deals and discounts, package bookings, and loyalty rewards.

3. TRANSPORTATION OPTIONS

- **Boise Airport (BOI)**

  - **Website**: iflyboise.com

  - **Overview**: Boise Airport is the primary gateway for air travel to the city. The airport's website provides information on flights, parking, ground transportation, and services.

  - **Resources**: Flight status updates, parking options, rental car information, and airport maps.

- **ValleyRide (Public Transportation)**

- Website: valleyregionaltransit.org

- Overview: ValleyRide offers public bus services throughout Boise and the surrounding areas. The website provides route maps, schedules, and fare information.

- Resources: Trip planner, real-time bus tracking, and service alerts.

- **Uber and Lyft**

  - Apps: Available on both iOS and Android

  - Overview: Ridesharing services like Uber and Lyft are widely available in Boise and are a convenient way to get around the city, especially for short trips.

  - Resources: Fare estimates, driver ratings, and real-time ride tracking.

- **Enterprise Rent-A-Car**

  - Website: enterprise.com

  - Overview: Enterprise offers a wide range of rental vehicles for exploring Boise and beyond. The company has multiple locations, including at Boise Airport.

  - Resources: Vehicle selection, online booking, and rental discounts.

4. LOCAL GUIDES AND APPS

- **Boise Weekly**

  - Website: boiseweekly.com

  - Overview: Boise Weekly is a local publication that provides news, events, and cultural insights. It's a great resource for finding out what's happening in the city during your visit.

- ○ **Resources**: Event listings, restaurant reviews, and arts and entertainment news.

- **Visit Idaho App**

  - ○ **Download**: Available on iOS and Android

  - ○ **Overview**: The Visit Idaho app offers an interactive guide to Boise and the rest of the state. It includes maps, travel guides, and event information.

  - ○ **Resources**: Trip planning tools, suggested itineraries, and offline access.

- **Yelp**

  - ○ **Website**: yelp.com

  - ○ **Overview**: Yelp is a popular platform for finding and reviewing local businesses, including restaurants, cafes, bars, and shops in Boise.

  - ○ **Resources**: User reviews, photos, and ratings to help you choose where to eat and shop.

5. EVENT CALENDARS AND TICKETING

- **Boise Events Calendar (Boise.org)**

  - ○ **Website**: boise.org/events

  - ○ **Overview**: This calendar lists upcoming events in Boise, including festivals, concerts, theater performances, and community events.

  - ○ **Resources**: Event descriptions, dates, times, and ticket information.

- **Eventbrite**

  - **Website**: eventbrite.com

  - **Overview**: Eventbrite is a platform for discovering and booking events in Boise, ranging from concerts and festivals to workshops and meetups.

  - **Resources**: Event searches by category, ticket purchasing, and event reminders.

- **Ticketmaster**

  - **Website**: ticketmaster.com

  - **Overview**: Ticketmaster is a leading platform for purchasing tickets to concerts, sports events, and theater performances in Boise.

  - **Resources**: Event listings, seat selection, and mobile ticketing.

6. *MAPS AND NAVIGATION*

- **Google Maps**

  - **Website**: maps.google.com

  - **Overview**: Google Maps is essential for navigating Boise, offering detailed maps, real-time traffic updates, and directions for driving, walking, biking, and public transit.

  - **Resources**: Street view, local business information, and custom map creation.

- **Boise City Map (City of Boise)**

  - **Website**: cityofboise.org/maps

- **Overview**: The City of Boise's official website offers downloadable maps, including bike paths, parks, and downtown Boise. It's a useful resource for getting oriented.

- **Resources**: Interactive maps, zoning maps, and public services information.

- **AllTrails**

  - **Website**: alltrails.com

  - **Overview**: AllTrails is a go-to resource for finding hiking and biking trails in and around Boise. It offers detailed trail maps, user reviews, and difficulty ratings.

  - **Resources**: Trail navigation, offline maps, and activity tracking.

7. CULTURAL AND HISTORICAL RESOURCES

- **Boise Art Museum**

  - **Website**: boiseartmuseum.org

  - **Overview**: The Boise Art Museum's website provides information on current exhibitions, educational programs, and special events.

  - **Resources**: Visitor information, membership details, and event calendars.

- **Idaho State Museum**

  - **Website**: history.idaho.gov/museum

  - **Overview**: The Idaho State Museum offers insights into Idaho's history and culture. The website includes information on exhibits, tours, and special events.

- **Resources**: Ticket purchasing, virtual exhibits, and educational resources.

- **Old Idaho Penitentiary**

  - **Website**: history.idaho.gov/old-idaho-penitentiary

  - **Overview**: This historic site's website provides details on tours, exhibits, and special events at the Old Idaho Penitentiary.

  - **Resources**: Visitor information, event tickets, and historical background.

8. SOCIAL MEDIA AND ONLINE COMMUNITIES

- **Instagram and Facebook**

  - **Profiles to Follow**:

    - @visitboise

    - @boiseweekly

    - @idahostatehistoricalsociety

  - **Overview**: Following these profiles on social media is a great way to stay updated on events, new attractions, and local insights. Many organizations and influencers share tips, photos, and recommendations.

- **Reddit - Boise Community**

  - **Website**: reddit.com/r/Boise

  - **Overview**: The Boise subreddit is an active online community where locals and visitors share information, ask questions, and discuss all things Boise.

- ○ **Resources**: Travel advice, restaurant recommendations, and local news.

CONCLUSION

As you've journeyed through the pages of this Boise Travel Guide 2025, you've likely discovered that Boise is not just another stop on the map—it's a destination that invites exploration, adventure, and a deep connection with both nature and community. From the moment you arrive, whether you're greeted by the vibrant arts scene or the rugged beauty of the surrounding foothills, Boise extends a warm and welcoming hand to every traveler.

A CITY OF CONTRASTS AND HARMONY

Boise is a city where contrasts coexist in perfect harmony. It's a place where the modern meets the historical, where innovation thrives alongside tradition, and where the bustling energy of urban life is tempered by the serene whispers of nature. Here, you can spend your morning hiking in the Boise Foothills, breathing in the crisp mountain air, and by afternoon, find yourself strolling through the vibrant streets of downtown, exploring local boutiques, sipping craft beer, or savoring farm-to-table cuisine.

The city's cultural tapestry is rich and diverse, woven from the threads of its Basque heritage, its pioneering history, and its ever-growing community of artists, musicians, and innovators. Whether you're exploring the murals of Freak Alley, enjoying a performance at the Boise Contemporary Theater, or simply chatting with locals at the farmers market, you'll find that Boise is a city that values creativity, expression, and the shared human experience.

SEASONS OF WONDER

Boise's appeal is ever-changing with the seasons, each bringing its own unique flavor to the city. Spring awakens the senses with blooming wildflowers and the gentle rush of the Boise River, perfect for outdoor enthusiasts who seek to hike, bike, or simply bask in the rebirth of nature. Summer stretches out long and golden, inviting you to float down the Boise River, enjoy outdoor concerts, and partake in the city's many festivals.

The warmth of the sun is matched only by the warmth of the community, as Boiseans come together to celebrate the season.

As autumn paints the city in shades of gold and crimson, the pace slows slightly, offering a perfect time for wine tasting in the Snake River Valley, enjoying the crisp air during a hike, or simply taking in the breathtaking fall foliage. Finally, winter brings a cozy charm to Boise, with snow-dusted streets, the allure of nearby ski slopes, and the festive lights that brighten the darkest nights. It's a time for bundling up, sipping hot cocoa, and experiencing the city's holiday spirit in all its glory.

A PLACE FOR EVERY TRAVELER

Boise is a city that truly has something for everyone. For the outdoor adventurer, the nearby mountains, rivers, and parks offer endless possibilities, from skiing and snowboarding at Bogus Basin to kayaking on the Boise River or exploring the vast wilderness of the Boise National Forest. For the culture enthusiast, the city's museums, galleries, and historic sites provide a deep dive into the art, history, and spirit of Idaho. Families will find a treasure trove of activities, from interactive exhibits at the Discovery Center of Idaho to the wildlife encounters at Zoo Boise.

Foodies will delight in Boise's culinary scene, where farm-to-table dining isn't just a trend but a way of life. The city's restaurants, cafes, and food trucks serve up a diverse array of flavors, all with a focus on fresh, local ingredients. And let's not forget the craft beer and wine enthusiasts— Boise's breweries and nearby vineyards are ready to welcome you with a pint or a glass of something special.

THE SPIRIT OF COMMUNITY

One of the most enduring aspects of Boise is its sense of community. The people of Boise, known for their friendliness and hospitality, make the city what it is. Whether you're attending a local festival, browsing through a neighborhood farmers market, or simply striking up a conversation with a local, you'll feel the strong community spirit that defines this city.

Boiseans are proud of their city, and they're eager to share it with you, making every visitor feel like part of the family.

LOOKING TO THE FUTURE

As Boise continues to grow and evolve, it remains deeply connected to its roots. The city is embracing the future with an eye toward sustainability, innovation, and inclusivity. As you explore Boise, you'll see the efforts to preserve its natural beauty, foster a thriving arts scene, and create a community that welcomes all. Whether you're visiting for the first time or returning to a city you love, Boise in 2025 promises new experiences, new connections, and new memories.

YOUR BOISE ADVENTURE AWAITS

So, as you close this guide and prepare for your Boise adventure, remember that this is just the beginning. Boise is a city that invites you to explore beyond the pages, to discover your own favorite spots, and to create your own stories. Whether you're here for a few days or a few weeks, Boise has a way of making you feel at home, while also inspiring you to see the world in a new light.

Pack your bags, bring your curiosity, and get ready to experience Boise—a city that's as welcoming as it is unforgettable. Whether you leave with souvenirs or simply memories, one thing is certain: Boise will leave an imprint on your heart, calling you back time and time again. Here's to your next great adventure in the City of Trees. Welcome to Boise, and enjoy the journey!

Made in the USA
Las Vegas, NV
14 February 2025

18141394R00125